Wind Energy Explained

A Simple Guide for Everyone

Nova Martian

Disclaimer

This book has been created with the assistance of AI tools for content generation, editing, and formatting. While AI tools have contributed to its development, the content has been reviewed to ensure its quality and accuracy. Readers are encouraged to approach the material critically and verify information where necessary.

Contents

Introduction

Wind energy stands as a beacon of innovation in the quest for sustainable and renewable power sources. As the world grapples with the pressing challenges of climate change and limited natural resources, the harnessing of wind energy offers a viable and increasingly popular solution. This book, "Wind Energy Explained: A Simple Guide for Everyone," seeks to provide a comprehensive yet accessible overview of wind energy, its significance, and its potential to reshape how we generate and consume electricity.

The rationale behind the growing interest in wind energy is multifaceted. It is one of the most environmentally friendly energy sources available, reducing reliance on fossil fuels and minimizing carbon emissions. Moreover, wind energy is abundant and inexhaustible, present in nearly every region around the globe. Its utility spans from massive power grids in developed countries to small-scale applications in remote areas. As technology advances, the efficiency and effectiveness of wind energy solutions continue to improve.

In this book, we will explore both the fascinating history and the cutting-edge technologies that define the wind energy sector today. Our goal is to unravel the complex mechanics of wind turbines, delve into the scientific principles of wind itself, and examine the different types of turbines and their applications. We will consider the manifold benefits of adopting wind energy, as well as the challenges that must be overcome to maximize its potential.

Furthermore, this book will address the crucial intersection of wind energy with environmental concerns, demonstrating how this renewable source can coexist with nature's ecosystems. We will also navigate through the landscape of policy and economics, highlighting how they shape the development and deployment of wind energy on a global scale. Finally, we will look toward the horizon, envisioning the future of wind energy and its pivotal role in a sustainable energy economy.

With this book, we aim to demystify the world of wind energy for the general reader, providing clarity and insight without sacrificing the depth and precision that the topic commands. Whether you are an environmental enthusiast, a student, a policymaker, or simply curious about the future of energy, this guide has been designed to equip you with a foundational understanding and inspire a deeper appreciation of wind power and its potential to drive a cleaner, greener future.

Chapter 1

Introduction to Wind Energy

Wind energy is a vital renewable resource that harnesses natural wind patterns to generate electricity. It offers a sustainable alternative to fossil fuels, with the growing global capacity illustrating its importance. By converting kinetic energy from the wind into usable electrical power, wind turbines contribute significantly to reducing carbon emissions. Understanding its mechanics and applications helps recognize its crucial role in advancing clean energy solutions worldwide.

1.1   Understanding Wind Energy

In an era where sustainability takes center stage, wind energy emerges as a beacon of hope. Harnessing the natural force of the wind is not a concept born in the modern world; rather, it is an idea steeped in centuries of human innovation. The importance of wind energy today, however, transcends its historical roots and opens a vital pathway toward carbon neutrality and energy security.

The Nature of Wind Energy. To appreciate wind energy, one must first embrace its elemental essence—a process whereby the kinetic energy from moving air is translated into electrical power through technologically advanced machinery. At its simplest, wind energy can be visualized as the symphony of aerodynamics made tangible through rotating turbines that convert motion into electrical current. This conversion process, elegantly demonstrated by both large-scale wind farms and compact residential turbines, offers a glimpse of a future less reliant on traditional fuels.

What sets wind energy apart is its renewable nature. Unlike fossil fuels, which deplete over time and contribute significantly to environmental pollution, wind is an inexhaustible resource. Fueled by the sun's heating of the Earth's surface and the planet's rotation, wind is a consistent yet variable force. As long as the sun shines and Earth spins, wind energy remains a viable and potent option for generating power.

Historical Perspectives. Wind energy is by no means a modern endeavor; its application stretches back to ancient civilizations who harnessed the wind for milling grain and pumping water. The iconic windmills of medieval Europe were technological marvels of their time, embodying the human spirit's desire to harness the earth's natural movements. Each towering windmill stood as a testament to understanding and utilizing wind to perform mechanical work—a concept that has evolved drastically to meet present-day needs.

Fast forward to the late 19th and early 20th centuries with the advent of electricity, which propelled wind energy into a new paradigm. Innovators such as Charles Brush and Poul la Cour began experimenting with wind turbine designs to generate electric power, when the vision of sprawling farms hosting countless wind turbines was little more than a figment of imagination.

The Modern Importance of Wind Energy. Today, wind energy holds significant status in global energy strategies. This is not merely due to its renewability but largely because of its environmental benefits and economic potential. Transitioning to wind energy contributes markedly to reducing greenhouse gas emissions, mitigating climate change impacts, and decreasing reliance on imported fuels.

Furthermore, wind energy projects create economic opportunities, driving job creation in manufacturing, installation, and maintenance sectors. Communities that once relied on traditional industries are finding new opportunities in wind energy, revitalizing local economies and supporting sustainable development.

The geographical omnipresence of wind also means energy diversification is possible in regions worldwide, improving resilience against supply disruptions. While some might argue about the intermittent nature of wind, modern solutions, such as energy storage systems and grid integration techniques, have made it feasible to accommodate these natural fluctuations.

Practical Applications and Future Innovations. Wind energy increasingly finds application in both residential settings and large-scale endeavors. Homeowners who appeal to sustainable practices often invest in small wind turbines, which can significantly offset household electricity costs and support local energy independence.

On a grander scale, towering offshore wind farms represent the cutting-edge frontier in wind energy technology. Such farms capitalize on steadier, stronger ocean winds to generate large quantities of electricity. Their placement offshore minimizes visual impact, avoids consuming valuable land, and opens up new expanses for energy harnessing.

As technology progresses, innovations such as floating wind turbines are set to revolutionize the field further.

These turbines can be deployed in deeper waters where wind resources are abundantly untapped. This innovation places humanity at the brink of a new era in wind energy utilization, continuously expanding the horizon of what is possible.

The Path Forward. With mounting pressures to address climate change and secure energy supplies, wind energy presents an imperative shift toward a sustainable future. The journey of wind energy, from humble grain mills to towering turbines in the midst of oceans, encapsulates not only humanity's engineering acumen but also a collective vision for a cleaner planet.

Future endeavors in wind energy must balance technological advancements with environmental and social considerations. This encompasses addressing challenges such as wildlife impact, community integration, and optimizing aesthetics.

Understanding wind energy is more than recognizing its mechanics and uses; it involves comprehending its critical role in our ongoing narrative towards sustainability. The endeavors of previous generations, coupled with today's innovations, light the path to a future where energy and environment harmoniously coexist, driven by the simple yet profound motion of the wind.

1.2   The Basics of Wind

Imagine standing on a hilltop as the wind whisks through your hair, and for a moment, you're privy to the invisible ballet that orchestrates one of nature's most intriguing phenomena. But what is wind, really? At its core, wind is simply air in motion, a dynamic occurrence fueled by the ceaseless energy of the sun. To unravel the enigma of wind, we must first dive into the intricate processes that lead to its formation, the forces that direct it, and the characteristics that define its essence.

The Birth of Wind

The story of wind begins with solar energy. The sun, our mighty star, doesn't distribute its warmth evenly across the Earth's surface. Variations in solar heating create areas of differing temperatures, which subsequently generate air pressure differentials. These differences in air pressure are the primary driving forces behind wind, compelling air to move from regions of higher pressure to those of lower pressure—a graceful odyssey set in motion by thermal disparities.

Consider the planet—one enormous thermodynamic playground where land and sea take turns absorbing and releasing the sun's energy. This leads to fascinating interactions: during the day, land heats up quicker than water, causing air over land to expand and rise, while cooler, denser air from the sea rushes inland to fill the void, forming a sea breeze. At night, the roles reverse with the land cooling faster, resulting in the creation of a land breeze. These diurnal cycles exemplify the small-scale, yet poignant, ballet of wind formation.

The Science of Wind Patterns

Understanding wind requires more than acknowledging its genesis; it demands a look at global factors influencing its flow, such as the Earth's rotation. Enter the Coriolis effect, a phenomenon arising from our planet's rotation. This invisible maestro bends wind paths, causing them to veer to the right in the Northern Hemisphere and to the left in the Southern Hemisphere. This deflection does not initiate wind, but it orchestrates its direction across vast expanses.

7

Prevailing wind patterns, known as trade winds, westerlies, and polar easterlies, emerge from the Coriolis effect combined with atmospheric convection cells. In tropical regions, trade winds sweep through, primary mechanisms that historically propelled merchant ships across oceans, a testament to the enduring relationship between humanity and wind. Westerlies dominate the mid-latitudes, shaping weather systems and steering the storms that water fields and fill reservoirs. In the polar regions, easterlies reign supreme, completing the atmospheric symphony.

Characteristics of Wind

Outside of scientific textbooks, wind is tangible and varied. Its characteristics—speed, direction, and constancy—form the backbone of weather forecasting and bear significant implications for wind energy applications.

Wind speed, measured in knots or meters per second, indicates the force and potential for energy extraction. In logistics, sailors have long depended on knowledge of wind speed for navigating oceans, while agriculturists see moderate winds as essential allies in pollinating crops.

Directionality, conveyed by meteorological instruments such as wind vanes, determines the wind's course. This becomes crucial when harnessing wind energy, as aligning turbines parallel to prevailing winds maximizes efficiency and power generation. For pilots, understanding wind direction is vital, allowing for smoother takeoffs and landings.

No less important is wind's consistency, or lack thereof. The unpredictability of wind may frustrate city-dwellers managing umbrellas on windy streets, yet it enriches the dynamics in sailboat racing, where adept sailors anticipate gusts to gain advantage. Stability—or volatility—of wind plays a pivotal role in siting wind turbines, particularly because fluctuations can affect both mechanical integrity and output reliability.

Wind in Cultural and Practical Contexts

Wind's presence is woven into the fabric of cultural consciousness. Poets often summon the image of a gentle breeze whispering of distant lands, an evocative metaphor for freedom and the unseen forces that influence life's voyage. In folklore, the wind bears messages from the gods, its invisible currents bridging the earthly and the celestial.

Practically, wind offers much more than romantic allusions; it is an agent of change and adaptation. Consider the ancient mariners, reliant on knowledge of the wind to cross uncharted waters. In agriculture, effective windbreaks—rows of trees or structures—help protect crops from damage, illustrating the harmonious coexistence with environmental forces.

More than ever before, the modern era sees wind guiding decisions of energy infrastructure. Countries invest heavily in wind forecasting models that scrutinize atmospheric data to optimize power generation and reduce dependency on fossil fuels. Tools like remote sensing devices and meteorological towers adorn landscapes, all in an effort to understand and predict wind's behavior for sustainable gain.

The Symphony of Wind

To comprehend wind is to grasp a piece of the Earth's breath, a vital element in the unbroken exchange between nature and society. Though invisible, wind imparts profound effects on energy, environment, and human existence. Its journey from heated ground to dynamic currents above manifests a tale deeply interconnected with life on Earth.

As we step onto the threshold of an eco-conscious future, recognizing wind in its natural and cultivated contexts allows us to appreciate its potential. Whether it brings the soft caress that cools summer evenings or powers turbines that light up towns and cities, wind remains an enduring reminder of our planet's beauty, its challenges, and above all, its possibilities.

1.3   Harnessing Wind Power

Standing on the brink of a new era in energy, one cannot overlook the elegant dance of the wind turbine—an engineering marvel that masterfully translates the kinetic ballet of air into the electrifying symphony of power. The story of capturing and converting wind energy is a tale of human ingenuity meeting nature's benign forces, a transformation as profound as it is complex.

From Breeze to Juice: The Turbine's Tale

Imagine a colossal pinwheel spinning gracefully against a blue sky. The modern wind turbine, reminiscent of a child's toy yet infinitely more sophisticated, sits at the heart of wind power electricity generation. Its blades, often spanning over a hundred meters in diameter, slice through the wind with precision born from meticulous design, harnessing energy that starts many miles away over the sun-warmed plains.

The turbine's rotors are the initial point of contact. With each rotation, the blades capture kinetic energy and rotate a shaft connected to a gear box. This gear box adjusts the slow, turning motion of the rotor into a much faster one suitable for electricity generation. At the journey's end lies an electrical generator which, like a modern-day alchemist, transforms kinetic motion into electrical currents ready to energize homes and industries alike.

This intricate process operates on the fundamental principles of electromagnetic induction: the generator spins a coil of wire within a magnetic field, inducing the flow of electricity. As direct descendants of those grain-grinding windmills from earlier centuries, today's turbines represent how far technology has come, innovating upon wind's raw potential with breathtaking efficiency.

Wind Farms: Harvesting Kinetics in Harmony

Although a standalone turbine offers a glimpse into the potentials of wind energy, the true marvel is observed in wind farms—vast stretches of land adorned with turbines like sentinels standing watch. Locations of these farms are no coincidence; they are carefully selected with the help of wind mapping and simulation models that identify sites with optimal wind speeds and consistency.

The siting of turbines is an art and science. Engineers and planners meticulously place turbines at specific intervals to maximize wind capture while minimizing turbulence from neighboring units. This careful choreography ensures that the energy extracted is at its zenith, and the site-specific microclimatic conditions help define regional installation patterns, whether they are laid inland, among hills, or offshore with panoramic seascapes.

Offshore Adventures: The Deepening Quest for Power

Crafting energy from wind farms on land is but one part of the picture. The oceans—with their strong, consistent winds and open expanses—offer a tantalizing venue for energy capture. Offshore wind farms, the modern titans of the seas, extend the reach of turbines into deeper

11

waters where winds blow unabated and the promise of power grows exponentially.

Offshore installations push technological innovation to new heights. Floating turbines, designed to withstand salt, sea, and storm, moor using cables anchored deep in the seabed. These hybrid structures represent the cutting edge of mechanical design and feasibility, posing unique challenges and opportunities.

By situating farms offshore, nations maximize their renewable energy potential while reducing the visual impact and land use conflicts that sometimes challenge onshore projects. The sheer output from these offshore giants is staggering too, with individual turbines producing enough energy to power thousands of homes.

Challenges: Taking the Wind Out of the Sails

As with all great endeavors, harnessing wind power comes with its own set of hurdles. Intermittency—the fluctuating nature of wind—remains a significant challenge. The wind does not always blow at speeds optimal for energy generation, which creates a variable supply in the electrical grid.

To counteract this, the integration of energy storage systems and grid improvements becomes vital. Batteries, compressed air, and even pumped hydro storage technologies provide adaptable solutions to balance these fluctuations, bridging gaps during stiller periods.

Moreover, environmental and aesthetic considerations play a pivotal role. Turbines can impact local ecosystems, prompting innovations in design to protect wildlife such as bats and birds from harm. Community engagement also remains integral, as projects strive for local acceptance through partnerships, benefit-sharing, and thoughtful site planning.

A Vision of the Future

Solar and wind are projected to dominate the clean energy sector in the coming decades, with wind energy poised to take center stage. As technology advances and costs continue to fall, the role of wind power in providing a sustainable energy future becomes increasingly indispensable.

Research accelerates; developments such as bladeless turbines, smart grid integrations, and AI-driven predictive maintenance offer tantalizing glimpses into a future where wind's full potential is harnessed more effectively and sustainably. On the horizon shines a world where the transition from a carbon-dependent energy model to a carbon-neutral one feels not just possible, but inevitable.

The journey from harnessing a simple breeze to transforming the energy landscape is a pivotal chapter not only for energy sciences but for humanity. For as long as the winds blow, the promise of sustainable energy generated from the Earth itself remains an astounding testament to human creativity and resilience. Through wind power, we are reminded of the harmonious partnership that can exist between nature's grace and humankind's enduring quest for innovation.

1.4 Global Wind Energy Capacity

In the panorama of renewable energy, wind power unfurls like a canvas splashed with potential and promise. As nations rally to decarbonize their energy systems, the global capacity of wind energy emerges as a measure of progress toward a cleaner future. But how has wind energy permeated the global landscape, and what does its distribution tell us about the commitment to sustainable power?

The Rise of Wind: A Global Dance

From the gusty plains of Texas to the offshore breezes of the North Sea, the evolution of wind energy paints a vivid picture. It speaks to the innovative spirit that has propelled turbines from niche projects to significant power providers, woven into grids across continents.

Globally, wind energy capacity has seen exponential growth over recent decades, an upward trajectory fueled by technological advances, policy support, and the pressing need to mitigate climate change. As technological prowess improved, the cost of wind energy plummeted, making it an increasingly viable option for both developed and emerging economies.

The statistic that stands at the forefront is global installed wind capacity, now surpassing 700 gigawatts, a figure illustrating considerable renewable penetration. This monumental capacity is not merely a number; it represents millions of turbines around the world, contributing a significant portion to the global energy mix, steadily closing the gap left by fossil fuels.

Leading the Charge: Champions of the Wind

Unsurprisingly, certain countries have taken the helm in the pursuit of wind energy. China leads the global pack, boasting the highest installed capacity, a result of its massive commitment to renewable infrastructure. China's wind farms, an extensive network of land-based and burgeoning offshore installations, symbolically reflect its strategy to curb air pollution and secure its energy independence.

In Europe, Germany, a staunch advocate for renewable energies, has transformed its landscape with synchronous rows of turbines, particularly in coastal regions. Germany's Energiewende, or energy transition policy, represents a profound shift towards sustainable energy, with wind power as a cornerstone of its strategy to achieve carbon neutrality.

The United States also plays a pivotal role, with vast expanses in states like Texas and Iowa dotted with turbines that paint a dynamic portrait of energy transition. American innovations in wind technology and policy frameworks have paved the way for significant private sector investment and expansion.

Wind Power in the Developing World

The adoption of wind energy is not confined to the wealthiest countries alone. Emerging economies recognize wind energy's potential as an antidote to energy poverty and a catalyst for sustainable development.

Consider India, a developing nation with ambitious wind capacity targets. As part of its commitment under the Paris Agreement, India is investing heavily in renewable energy to power its rapidly growing population sustainably. Wind farms sprout across the Indian subcontinent, powering homes, businesses, and industries with green energy.

Similarly, in Africa, countries like South Africa and Kenya are tapping into their wind resources. Projects such as the Lake Turkana Wind Power project in Kenya— the largest wind farm on the continent—highlight the tenacity to harness natural resources in regions often reliant on fossil imports. This shift is not just an energy story; it's a narrative of empowerment and local self-reliance.

Challenges and Opportunities

Despite its growth, the deployment of wind energy comes with a plethora of challenges and opportunities. One major hurdle is integration into existing energy systems, which were predominantly designed for steady, controllable power sources. The variability and intermittency of wind require smart grids and energy storage solutions to ensure a reliable supply.

Additionally, there's the issue of land use and environmental considerations. Ensuring that wildlife habitats are preserved and that local communities benefit economically from wind projects remains a balancing act. Social acceptance is therefore critical, necessitating transparency and engagement with local populations.

Conversely, the benefits offer ample reasons for optimism. Investment in wind energy creates jobs, fosters technological innovation, and drives economic growth. Moreover, it represents a commitment to a sustainable future, cutting emissions and steering the global ship toward a viable climate future.

The Roadmap Ahead

Looking forward, the global wind energy sector is poised for further expansion, driven by policy commitments, technological advancements, and an increasing awareness of the climate imperative. The imagined future is one of collaboration—nations working together through shared innovation and technology transfer to optimize wind resources globally.

Offshore wind holds particular promise, with plans for extensive expansion in Europe, Asia, and even the United States. The development of floating wind platforms is expected to unlock vast water-based resources, paving the way for the next big leap in wind capacity.

Globally, the ambition is clear: to harness the full potential of wind energy, mastering nature's currents to generate energy sustainably and equitably. In doing so, every turbine turned by the wind speaks to a world eager to embrace the power of its natural heritage, forging ahead to secure a climate-friendly energy paradigm that benefits the globe in equal measure.

1.5   Wind Energy in Everyday Life

Picture the landscape of a small town, church steeples standing tall, while the horizon teases of distant fields adorned with sleek wind turbines. These structures, once the preserve of distant, rural settings, increasingly populate our everyday surroundings, emblematic of the quiet but profound revolution in how we perceive and utilise energy. Wind energy, harnessed in earnest, permeates our daily lives more than one might envision, transforming how societies operate and connect with the natural world.

Power to the People

Let's begin with the most straightforward element: electricity in our homes and workplaces. The flick of a switch, a gesture so mundane, is imbued with significance when we note the source of the power that illuminates our lives. Thanks to modern advances, a considerable portion of this electricity now flows from the gentle churn of wind turbine blades, contributing to the grid's supply in ways that are both sustainable and reliable.

In cities across the globe, one can find homes and businesses powered entirely by renewable energy packages—wind energy often being a pivotal component. Whether charging our myriad devices, brewing a morning cup of coffee, or even savoring an evening's warmth beneath a cozy lamp, wind energy quietly imbues our daily rituals with a touch of the ethical, contributing to a cleaner atmosphere and a reduction in fossil fuel dependency.

On a personal scale, the zero-emissive characteristic of wind energy bolsters societal efforts to lower carbon footprints. A reduction in individual and collective environmental impact finds growing appeal among consumers, as green energy tariffs become not only feasible but desirable choices.

Empowering Communities and Fuelling Change

Beyond individual benefit, wind energy serves as a keystone to community empowerment. Localized wind farms often become community projects in themselves, where profits are reinvested into local infrastructure, schools, and renewable endeavors. The financial boon from selling excess energy back to the grid enriches municipalities while providing job opportunities in operation, maintenance, and educational outreach.

An intriguing example lies in microgrids, particularly in settings that dare to dream of self-sufficiency. These smaller, localized power systems rely on wind, coupled with other renewable sources, to meet energy requirements independently of large networks. Island communities or remote areas, often at the mercy of costly and ecologically damaging diesel imports, find in wind energy a sustainable path toward energy security and resilience.

Furthermore, wind energy becomes a crucial tool for infrastructures transitioning from fossil fuels towards renewables. Modern initiatives aim for energy democracy—empowering local stakeholders—and wind power forms a vital component of decentralized energy solutions that put control back into the hands of

18

the community.

Wind for All Seasons: Energy in Public and Private Spaces

The ballet of wind energy extends beyond the grid and the meter box. Urban planners and architects have begun to weave wind energy into the very fabric of cityscapes. Designs incorporate building-integrated turbines—vertical-axis models tailored to harness winds that skirt across rooftops and alleys—integrating aesthetics with function in a symbiotic relationship between nature and construction.

Public transport systems, too, glean tidy gains from wind energy. Electrified transport networks, including trams and subway systems, increasingly rely on renewable streams to keep the wheels turning and the lights on. This transition reveals a modal shift in thinking, beyond merely providing transportation, to aligning with broader sustainability goals.

On the horizon, electric vehicles (EVs) emerge as key players in the green transition. As charging infrastructures continue to expand, often supplied by renewable sources, EVs move ever closer to becoming true champions of sustainable commuting. A wind-powered car charger epitomizes entwined progress, traversing roads courtesy of an energy source that starts its journey far above in the azure sky.

Wind's Whisper: Innovations and Future Directions

Wind energy's relevance does not culminate in the present; rather, it whispers of future trends and advancements. Urban substations adorned with microturbines, data centers cooled and powered by offshore wind, and even agriculture—where autonomous drones, integral for precision farming, are recharged by mobile wind stations—paint a vibrant tapestry of integration.

Efforts in hybrid systems showcase burgeoning overlaps between wind and solar, storage solutions, and even biogas, forming symbiotic ecosystems where each component enhances overall efficiency and adaptability. These initiatives spark a burgeoning dialogue between technology and environment, casting wind energy as a reliable partner in an interconnected energy landscape.

As we edge forward, the adaptation of AI and machine learning for predictive maintenance and efficiency optimization promises to enhance the reliability and lifespan of wind assets. Wind farms, both terrestrial and maritime, will evolve into smart systems, with coordinated turbines communicating and adapting to environmental stimuli on-the-fly, learning from observations accumulated over time.

The Breath of Progress

In recounting the tale of wind energy in everyday life, we observe a breath of progress filling our sails with aspiration. Far from mere apparatuses on the skyline, turbines represent a foundation for progressive change and communal resilience. Through teaching future generations and integrating seamlessly into our lives, wind energy embodies a broader commitment to sustainable practice, echoing its quiet strength throughout society.

It's not simply that we harness the wind's power, but that its very presence underscores humankind's potential to thrive alongside nature. Wind energy invites us to reconsider our relationship with the environment, to follow currents of change towards a sustainable tomorrow, and ultimately, to listen as the wind murmurs to us a story of infinite possibilities.

Chapter 2

History of Wind Power

Wind power has evolved from ancient sailboats and windmills to modern turbines driving electricity generation. Throughout history, innovations during the medieval period and the Industrial Revolution have significantly advanced wind technology. The 20th century saw substantial growth, leading to today's sophisticated systems. This historical progression underscores wind power's enduring relevance and its transformation into a key player in sustainable energy solutions.

2.1   Early Uses of Wind Power

The story of wind power begins thousands of years ago, when ancient civilizations first harnessed the invisible force of moving air. In a time where natural elements dictated the rhythms of life, the wind was both relentless and reliable. Its utilization for sailing and grinding grains marks some of humanity's earliest attempts to derive energy from the natural world. In this section, we embark on a journey through time, exploring how ancient societies tapped into this potent resource, laying a foundation for future technological advances.

Imagine the vast desert landscapes of ancient Egypt or the open seas near the Aegean Islands. In these settings, the wind was more than just a force of nature—it was an ally in survival and a catalyst for travel and commerce.

One of the most significant early applications of wind power was in sailing. Long before complicated machines transformed energy, the simple sailboat stands as a classic example of ingenious design meeting environmental necessity. The earliest evidence of sailing can be traced back to the Egyptians around 3000 BCE. They crafted simple boats with square sails, using reed and wood, which allowed them to navigate the River Nile efficiently. These vessels brought goods, such as grains and stones, essential for constructing their iconic monuments, upgrading the scope of trade and cultural exchange.

The exploration of wind power through sailing continued to evolve, dramatically influencing the cultures that embraced it. The Phoenicians, known as the formidable sailors of antiquity, looked beyond coastal routes, venturing into open waters. Their advanced shipbuilding techniques included the development of more sophisticated rigging systems that permitted traversal across the Mediterranean Sea, opening expansive trade networks that significantly impacted the economic and cultural landscapes of that era.

While sailing empowered these ancient peoples to extend their horizons, wind found a second life on land. Imagine the rhythmic clunk of a grindstone turning in a brisk breeze—an auditory reminder of how the power of nature has long been a companion in the labor of daily life. Windmills may first bring to mind picturesque Dutch landscapes, but their origins reach back to Persian innovations around 200 BCE. This ingenious design utilized vertical-axis windmills constructed mainly of bundled reeds or wood.

These early windmills powered simple machinery to grind grains, crucial for maintaining sustenance in agrarian societies. By transforming crops like wheat and barley into flour, these mechanisms revolutionized food production, enabling communities to store substantial food supplies, thereby enhancing stability and self-sufficiency.

From Persia, the concept of windmills traversed to China and the Indian subcontinent. In China, wind was one of the "Four Heavenly Forces," and its role in mechanizing intensive labor showcases an early appreciation for efficient technology. Chinese wind-powered mechanisms were known less for grinding grains and more for irrigation, illustrating practicality catered to specific regional demands.

As trade routes expanded, so too did knowledge. The journey of windmill technology to Europe during the medieval period illustrates the profound interconnectedness of ancient societies. European adaptations saw notable evolution in the design—the post and tower mills exemplified architectural ingenuity that would later influence Western industrialization.

The wind's untamed spirit, harnessed by these early civilizations, is a testament to human curiosity and adaptability. Sailing empowered societies to cross new frontiers, while windmills mechanized agriculture and sustained growing populations. In both cases, the ability to utilize wind laid the groundwork for significant socioeconomic development, forging a pathway toward further technological exploration.

As we reflect on these seminal uses of wind, it is worth considering how these ancient applications inform modern wind technology. The basic principles remain strikingly similar—utilizing wind to produce kinetic energy, serving both human needs and furthering progress. Yet, from simple sails and humble mills, we now stand amidst towering turbines, perpetuating a tradition rooted in our earliest encounters with the elements.

In contemplating early uses of wind power, we appreciate that today's innovations are not abrupt intrusions into a natural world but rather continuations of a dialogue begun with the first human hand raised to feel the breeze. The history encapsulates a deeper understanding of wind's potential—a dynamic force that, when paired with human creativity, transforms both lives and landscapes.

2.2   The Advent of Windmills

As the world transitioned from ancient to medieval times, the whispers of change echoed across Europe. Societies were reshaping themselves—economies were growing, populations expanding, and the medieval mind was ever inquisitive about novel ways to harness the omnipresent elements. Among these transformations stood the evolution of windmills, not merely as machines but as milestones in the rippling journey towards technological prowess.

Imagine a European landscape, where fields stretch on, dotted with villages. At the heart of these settlements, the rotating vanes of rudimentary windmills began to appear, marking a shift in how communities approached harnessing wind energy. The arrival of windmills during the medieval period was marked by regional styles and practical innovations that testified to local customs and needs, serving as symbols of both ingenuity and practical enterprise.

The artistry of medieval windmills began with the post mill, a design that emerged around the 12th century. The post mill boasted a lightweight construction allowing the entire structure to turn to face the wind. Built around a central vertical post, these windmills epitomized simplicity and utility. A typical post mill consisted of a wooden construction with a small enclosure containing milling apparatus atop a single large post. The innovation lay in the ability to pivot the windmill with the changing wind direction, achieved through pushing a long tail attached to the rear, or in more advanced designs, with a winding gear system. This adaptability granted post mills a broad operational capacity across various terrains with swirling wind conditions.

The spread of post mills throughout northern Europe demonstrated a pragmatic response to the availability of resources and the sociopolitical conditions of the time. As these mills populated the landscape, their utility became woven into the fabric of daily life, driving meal preparation by grinding grains, drawing water, and even sawing wood—each advancement further ingraining windmills into economic and cultural life.

As time progressed, the sophisticated designs of tower mills arose, marking a pivotal leap forward. Unlike their predecessors, tower mills featured a stationary base, often cylindrical, crafted from stone or brick, with only the cap supporting the sails capable of rotation. This not only enhanced the structural integrity, making them less susceptible to the ravages of turbulent weather, but also maximized the efficiency of capturing wind from all directions, as the cap could be rotated to follow the prevailing winds.

Dutch engineering prowess led to transformative tower mill innovations in the 14th and 15th centuries. The multi-story design integrated storage and additional operational capabilities like pumping water—a critical function in the battle against the encroaching sea. The polders, low-lying tracts of land reclaimed from the sea in the Netherlands, exhibit the power of wind-driven irrigation as an agent of survival and progress, turning potential calamity into cultivation grounds.

Windmills during the medieval period were more than economic engines; they were reflections of the societal structures that built them. The control and operation of windmills were often central to community governance. Laws and rights related to windmills were established, defining ownership models, such as the feudal system where windmills commonly belonged to landlords and local nobility. These properties exemplified the inter-section of power and technology as millers became key figures, straddling the line between skilled tradesmen and socio-economic intermediaries, positioned by virtue of their proximity to these valued machineries.

Cross-cultural exchanges along trade routes further facilitated the dissemination of windmill technology. Innovation was not insular but rather a blending of ideas and techniques. The Crusades, with their cross-pollination of cultures, played a notable role in spreading windmill technology from Europe to the Middle East and vice versa, showcasing how the movement of ideas often outpaces the trajectory of armies.

In examining windmills, we see an evolution concurrent with medieval society itself—craft and art flourishing under the winds of change. The tops of these monumental constructs spun round the clock, underscoring humanity's endless quest to gather, refine, and use natural forces to its advantage. From the humble post mill to the grandiose tower mill, these windmills left indelible imprints not just on landscapes but also on the cultures that built them.

Without peering through the lens of historical context and embracing the story of windmills, one might overlook how their advent served as a foothold, leading toward modern wind-powered advancements. In a world today where sleek, towering turbines dominate discussions about renewable energy, a thread can be traced back to these mechanical sentinels of the past, melding the agricultural with the architectural in a legacy that still catches the wind as it always has, urging us forward.

2.3 Wind Power in the Industrial Age

As the curtain rose on the Industrial Revolution, a period marked by dramatic shifts and strenuous advances, the landscape of energy consumption began to radically transform. Yet, amid the clatter of steam engines and the rise of coal as a dominant force, wind power—buoyant and venerable—continued to carve its niche. This era illuminated not just a recalibration of natural forces, but also a profound realignment of human ingenuity in adapting an ancient power source to meet the escalating demands of an industrious age.

The Industrial Revolution, beginning in the late 18th century, was characterized by a thirst for energy unprecedented in human history. As industries burgeoned, so too did the requisite energy needed to propel machinery and production. Amidst this, wind power proved invaluable, particularly in applications that its new fossil fuel rivals were less equipped to address.

While steam lent its brawn to industrial machinery, windmills remained steadfast allies in agriculture and rural communities—areas less electrified by change. It is here that wind reasserted its relevance.   Its role in mechanizing tasks, such as water pumping, served to irrigate vast stretches of farmland.   The iconic windpump, a descendant of earlier windmill technologies, rose to prominence, especially across the windswept plains of the Netherlands and the remote expanses of the American Midwest.

The American windpump, with its skeletal metal structure and multi-bladed fan, painted an iconic silhouette against the sky.   This evolution underscored the adaptation of wind power to the new realities of industrial agriculture, assisting the relentless push of westward expansion.   In a sense, these windpumps became pivotal in 'taming' the wilderness, enabling new settlement patterns by providing the lifeline of water to arid lands.

As urban centers grew, harnessing wind power in ways previously unimaginable became tantalizing. In the mid-19th century, urban planning began to recognize the aesthetic and utilitarian merits of wind.   Projects emerged that sought to integrate wind-driven structures within the burgeoning cityscape, providing a vision where energy generation could harmonize with human habitat.

Across the Atlantic, Europe, too, explored new applications for wind.   Nations with seafaring legacies like Britain and Denmark envisioned wind power in maritime contexts, with experiments in wind-powered propulsion systems to complement traditional sails. Though steamship technology quickly overshadowed these innovations, the exploration seeded ideas that would later inspire and revive interest in renewable maritime propulsion.

Arguably, the most significant leap in understanding wind during this era was the conceptual shift in

28

energy recognition and distribution. Innovators acknowledged that harnessing wind meant more than merely supplementing energy needs—it symbolized a vital diversification of energy sources that could hedge against the uncertainties of relying solely on coal and steam. Ecological foresight began to bloom; wind was not just seen as a relic of agrarian past but as a cornerstone of sustainable practice.

Experiments in electrical generation gradually interwove with the utilization of wind during this time. In 1887, James Blyth, a Scottish engineer, erected perhaps the world's first wind turbine for electricity production. His modest turbine powered his holiday home in Marykirk, Aberdeen, offering proof-of-concept that hinted at windswept electricity's vast potential. Further south, in Denmark, Poul la Cour—often dubbed the father of modern wind power—undertook pivotal experiments in the late 19th century, enhancing turbine efficiency and refining the transmission of generated power.

This budding interplay between wind and electricity laid foundational stones for what would burgeon in the 20th century, but its roots remained firmly in industrial-era explorations. Through these endeavours, wind power metamorphosed from bucolic support to a contender in electrical technology, foreshadowing its modern resurgence.

The Industrial Age thus tells a story not only of shift but also of resilience, revealing how wind's timeless dance persisted amidst the fervor of industrialization. It wasn't merely a candle holding against the storm of mechanization, but rather a persistent ally—the familiar old friend satisfying niche roles while tentatively venturing into the uncharted potential of generating the very lifeblood of modern society: electricity.

Wind power's adaptation during the Industrial Revolution signifies more than mere continuity; it represents an era wherein humanity began recognizing the vast potential inherent in this abundant natural force. As the world plowed forward, wind quietly yet steadfastly fueled progress, reminding us even amidst the most transformative of times, the whisper of the wind maintains its enchanting promise for the ages.

2.4   20th Century Innovations

The 20th century was a period defined by breathtaking technological advancements and transformations across the globe. Within this vibrant tapestry of innovation, wind energy began to emerge from its pre-industrial past to take on a more modern guise. From quirky experiments to serious engineering feats, the 1900s bore witness to wind's rebirth amidst evolving energy demands.

In the early part of the century, the appeal of wind energy lay primarily in its inexhaustible potential and the specter of an oil-dependent future—an early harbinger of today's energy anxieties. This period marked a time when societies started to critically evaluate the sustainability of their energy sources, making wind an attractive, though initially niche, proposition.

The notions of harnessing wind's energy for electricity— first experimented with on a small scale in previous centuries—garnered attention with an enthusiastic optimism. The landscape of renewable energy was akin to the wild west, where wind pioneers wielded wits and wrenches more than they relied on established wisdom.

One of the pioneering efforts in the utilization of wind for electricity was the construction of the first modern wind turbine in 1931 in Yalta, by the USSR. With rotors spanning 30 meters, this trailblazer generated 100 kW of power, proving that wind could be captured on a scale substantial enough to feed into a centralized power grid. This initiative inspired further experimentation and enthusiasm worldwide.

In Denmark, a country with a longstanding heritage of windmill innovation, additional strides were being made. In 1957, the Gedser wind turbine, designed by Johannes Juul, offered a glimpse of future potential. Its three-bladed design became a precursor to modern turbine structures, operating successfully until the mid-1960s and influencing future developments in wind energy.

Across the Atlantic, efforts in harnessing wind for electricity saw significant leaps as well. Stormy insights into petroleum's environmental costs, coupled with the swirling economic gusts of the 1970s oil crises, prompted a renewed commitment to exploring alternative energy sources in the United States. In this tense energy environment, California established itself as a hotbed for wind energy initiatives. The California Wind Energy Projects of the 1980s, spurred by federal and state-level incentives, were monumental. They transformed the wind-laden terrain of regions like Altamont Pass into sprawling landscapes of modern wind farms, giving the turbine-dotted skyline its unmistakable signature.

Wind technology designs during this era took on increasingly sophisticated forms. The transition from experimental single turbines to large-scale wind farms was facilitated by improvements in materials, aerodynamics, and overall design efficiency. Wind turbine blades began to resemble aircraft wings—slender and elegantly optimized to extract maximum energy from the moving air.

The cultural and technological backdrop of the 20th century's later decades presented both opportunities and challenges for wind energy's advocates. With growing public awareness of environmental issues, wind energy found itself in the middle of a burgeoning ecological discussion about reducing carbon emissions and advancing sustainable practices.

In this century of unprecedented technological development, wind's potential as a clean, renewable energy source became embedded in national energy policies. By the century's close, European and North American nations invested heavily in research and incentives, prompting a proliferation of wind farm developments. This institutional investment was driven not only by ecological idealism but also by a pragmatic recognition of wind power's long-term economic viability.

Wind energy's journey through the 20th century was not just a tale of mechanical and electrical achievement, but also a narrative deeply entwined with evolving environmental ideologies. The crisscrossing threads of geopolitical calculations, economic strategy, and technological possibility created a broader understanding of wind's role in the energy matrix.

Today, reflecting on the 20th century's innovations fosters a deep appreciation of wind energy's steady ascent. From singular turbines humming alone on remote landscapes to integrated grids of thousands generating power for millions, wind's transformation mirrors humanity's own quest for sustainable progress. As we navigate the complexities of 21st-century energy needs, the legacy of 20th-century innovations charts a course for the future—one shaped as much by the wind as it is by the hands that strive to harness it.

2.5 Modern Wind Power

As we sail into the 21st century, the realm of wind power stands at the forefront of technological innovation and environmental pragmatism. The gentle breath of ancient winds has evolved into a vibrant force of modernity, now harnessing nature's invisible currents to light up cities and power industries. Modern wind power is not just a technical marvel but also a symbol of a global shift toward sustainable energy and a reflection of our ongoing commitment to curbing climate change.

Central to this transformation is the technological sophistication of wind turbines. Once modest constructions on pastoral fields, wind turbines today have become engineering juggernauts, towering as high as skyscrapers, with blades that sweep elegantly across the sky like immense kinetic sculptures. The latest advancements in turbine design focus on maximizing efficiency, ensuring that every gust of wind is captured with optimal efficacy. State-of-the-art materials, such as advanced composites for blade construction, enhance durability and reduce weight, thereby enhancing performance while minimizing maintenance.

Furthermore, wind energy technology has undergone a digital revolution. Smart turbines, equipped with sensors and data analytics capabilities, adjust their operations in real time based not only on wind speed and direction but also on predictive maintenance schedules and grid demands. These intelligent systems allow for turbines to operate more efficiently and with greater reliability than ever before, driving down costs and increasing their attractiveness to investors.

Geographical expansion has also played a crucial role in modern wind power. Offshore wind farms represent one of the most ambitious frontiers. Unlike their land-based predecessors, offshore turbines benefit from the stronger and more consistent winds available at sea. Projects such as the Hornsea Project in the North Sea are leading the charge, setting records for both size and power output. Offshore developments also mitigate common land-based concerns, such as noise and aesthetic impact, while supporting significant power generation capabilities.

Moreover, the environmental consciousness that propels modern wind energy has catalyzed efforts to integrate wind farms into existing ecological and social landscapes harmoniously. By engaging with communities and adopting environmentally sensitive designs, wind projects ensure that renewable energy production can coexist with conservation and cultural heritage. Collaborative efforts with environmental organizations have led to improved strategies for minimizing impacts on local wildlife, particularly regarding avian species, which often face significant risks from turbine blades.

From a policy perspective, governments worldwide are increasingly recognizing the imperatives of transitioning to low-carbon energy systems. Incentives, subsidies, and long-term vision frameworks have expanded the horizon for wind power, driving significant investment and innovation in this sector. The burgeoning global market shares in wind energy create a positive feedback loop, encouraging further competitiveness and technological advancements.

While economic viability remains paramount, the scale and scope of modern wind power projects are ambitious. The synergy between wind and other renewable energy sources—such as solar and energy storage technologies—illustrates a future where diverse yet harmonious energy solutions work in concert to meet global needs. For example, hybrid renewable systems combine wind and solar power to compensate for periods when one resource is less available, thereby ensuring a more stable supply of electricity.

Perhaps one of the most compelling aspects of modern wind power is its role in the democratization of energy. Small-scale wind projects are sprouting in regions traditionally disconnected from centralized grids. In regions where electrification is nascent, small turbines power homes, schools, and clinics, fundamentally altering development trajectories. They provide not just electricity, but empower communities towards sustainable development, enhancing education, healthcare, and economic growth.

Modern wind power illustrates a profound narrative: one of balance, empowerment, and responsibility. It underscores our journey from relying on the caprice of the elements to mastering them through elegant solutions. The whispers of the wind are now robust dialogues, engaging all of humanity in a quest for a greener, brighter future. With every turn of a blade, we edge closer to sustainable prosperity, proving that the wind is, indeed, a friend worth keeping.

Chapter 3

How Wind Turbines Work

Wind turbines capture kinetic energy from the wind through rotor blades, converting it into mechanical power. This mechanical energy is then transformed into electricity via a generator. The electricity is transmitted to the grid for distribution. Factors such as turbine components, design, and site conditions influence their efficiency. Understanding these processes highlights the complexity and effectiveness of wind turbines in generating clean energy.

3.1 Components of a Wind Turbine

In the serene stretch of landscapes punctuated by the quiet elegance of wind farms, the wind turbine stands as a stalwart sentinel, capturing the whispers of the wind and transforming them into the powerful hum of electrical energy. At its heart, the turbine is a symphony of engineering prowess, with each component playing a crucial role in this harmonious conversion of kinetic energy to electrical power. Every element, from the aerodynamic blades to the intricate workings of the nacelle, is a testament to ingenuity and precision.

Let us first turn our attention to the blades of a wind turbine, arguably the most iconic and visible part.

These blades serve as the primary interface between nature's gusty offerings and the mechanical innards of the turbine.   Typically, a wind turbine features three large blades, reminiscent of an airplane propeller, each elegantly shaped to maximize efficiency through aerodynamic optimization.   This design concept, akin to that used in aircraft wings, exploits the principles of lift and drag. As the wind flows over the curved surface of the blades, it generates a difference in pressure that causes the rotor to spin. It is a mesmerizing dance with the natural elements, whereby even a gentle breeze can set the massive blades in motion.

Historically, evolving from Dutch windmills to the sleek turbines of today, blade materials have transitioned from wood to metal, and now predominantly composite materials.   Modern turbine blades are constructed from fiberglass-reinforced polyester or epoxy, carefully engineered to balance strength, weight, and durability. This adherence to materials science ensures that they can withstand the relentless forces of nature.   Some of the largest blades exceed 80 meters in length, designed to capture more wind and thus more energy.   As an illustrative example, consider a blade gently slicing through the air like a chef's knife through soft butter, driven by nothing but invisible wind currents.

Central to the movement of the blades is the rotor, comprising the hub and the attached blades.   The hub serves as the core connection point, where the blades secure their positions and synchronize to turn in unison. Within this windy orchestra, the rotor's role is indispensable.   It acts like the conductor, initiating the mechanical processes that follow.   Here lies the critical conversion of wind to rotational energy—a process marked by meditative grace.

Moving onward, let us venture into the nacelle, a robust

housing located atop the turbine tower. While the blades and rotor delicately interact with the elements outside, the nacelle contains the turbine's complex systems, hidden yet fundamental. It is within this aerodynamic enclosure that the kinetic energy from the spinning rotor is transformed into mechanical energy, and subsequently, electrical energy. Among the various components housed within the nacelle, the gearbox stands out as a pivotal player. Like an industrious intermediary, the gearbox increases the slow rotational speed of the rotor to a much higher rate suitable for generating electrical power in the turbine's generator.

Thanks to sophisticated engineering, the nacelle balances mechanical functionality with protection. It shields vital components such as the generator, gearbox, and control systems from environmental exposures. Imagine it as the turbine's operational brain, orchestrating the conversion processes with meticulously scheduled precision. Furthermore, the nacelle is equipped with sensors and control mechanisms, allowing it to rotate, or yaw, to face the direction of the wind. This dynamic adjustment ensures optimal performance and energy capture at all times, a marvel of automation akin to a sailor adjusting a vessel's sails to harness the wind most efficiently.

The technological sophistication extends even to monitoring. Within the nacelle, sensors constantly relay data, reflecting the omnitasking brain of the turbine, tirelessly changing the pitch of the blades and adjusting operations to maximize energy efficiency and ensure safety.

As we delve further into each component, the scale and dexterity of these marvels become apparent. Each blade, rotor movement, gearbox gearing, and electrical generation component resonates with engineering harmony, displaying innovation spun from the winds of time and progress. A wind turbine, therefore, is not merely a mechanical structure, but a dynamic entity, constantly interacting with its environment and adapting to the caprices of the wind while steadfastly producing clean energy.

In considering the components of a wind turbine, we appreciate the careful amalgam of design, material science, and engineering that allows these silent giants to convert wind's whispers into the symphony of sustainable energy. It is a testament to human ingenuity—a modern-day homage to the age-old alliance between humankind and the natural power of the wind.

3.2   The Mechanics of Wind Energy

In the vast and unending conversation between the Earth and the skies, wind energy stands out as a quiet yet powerful voice. It's the very art of utilizing movement that transforms invisible streams of air into tangible forms of power. But how exactly does a wind turbine perform this remarkable magic trick of changing wind into mechanical energy?

The journey begins with understanding the fundamental nature of wind itself—a vast, untapped reservoir of kinetic energy. Wind results from the sun's uneven heating of the Earth's surface. This variance causes air to move from high-pressure areas to low-pressure regions, creating the winds that have shaped both our physical landscapes and human history. Harnessing this energy, then, was merely a matter of time and ingenuity.

The key element in this energetic transference is the rotor blades of a wind turbine, akin to open arms eagerly awaiting the wind's embrace. As the wind hits the blades, it splits, with some of it passing over the curved top and some below. Thanks to Bernoulli's principle, this setup creates a pressure differential, with higher pressure below and lower above, generating lift—the same principle enabling aircraft to soar. Ingeniously, the blades are crafted to exploit this lift efficiently, not for flight, but for rotation. Thus, when wind imparts enough force, the blades begin to turn, setting in motion the symphony of energy conversion.

At the heart of this operation is the rotor—a captivating blend of physics and motion, where the space between the blades and hub becomes a canvas for the science of aerodynamics. As the blades spin, they carry the rotor into their dance, twisting and turning with an elegance only nature can inspire. It is a stunning rebirth of wind into torque—a twisting force that is the first step in siphoning nature's gift into usable mechanical energy.

Progressing further into the mechanical belly of the turbine, this newfound rotational energy seeks its next purpose. Enter the eminent gearbox, stationed like a diligent worker, tirelessly shifting gears. Most wind turbines are equipped to accelerate slow rotational speeds to the level where electricity generation becomes feasible, converting the energy into a faster rotational form within the confines of the nacelle. Picture the gearbox as a humble artisan transforming a basic material into an intricate masterpiece—indeed, it speeds up the leisurely pace of the rotor's turn to a brisk spin necessary for the generator.

This mechanical marvel does not operate alone; it stands as part of a lineage of innovation. Historically, the journey from rudimentary windmills to modern turbines encapsulates human ambition and adaptability. Ancient civilizations, from the Persians to the Dutch, all discovered variations of utilizing wind's kinetic energy long before today's refined machinery took shape. In medieval Europe, the iconic windmills played a vital role in agricultural productivity, transforming grain into flour with the persistent push of the wind.

Returning to present-day technology, the dynamic dance of energy changes tempo inside the nacelle. Here we witness the cunning of engineering—turning wind-borne rotational energy into centralized mechanical power.   The mechanical intricacy doesn't just end there; there is yet more choreography as sensors and computer systems constantly listen, adjust, and improve performance.   They provide a modern twist, literally and figuratively, as they adjust the positioning of blades and the yaw of the nacelle to optimize energy capture throughout the day, adapting to variable wind speeds and directions.

Understandably, the conversion process does more than capture energy; it represents humanity's drive to cultivate a sustainable future.   As fossil fuels retreat further into history's shadows, wind energy steps forward, promising a cleaner, greener power source with mechanical processes at its core.   Innovation continually pushes boundaries—smarter materials, adaptive technologies, and imaginative solutions blossom from academic thesis to industrial application.

In actual applications, consider a coastal wind farm: powerful sea breezes spin turbines that tower over the landscape, their silhouettes immortalized against blazing sunsets.   The rotational energy generated cascades into regional power grids, providing homes with clean energy and reducing carbon footprints, all thanks to the mechanical wizardry at play within each turbine.

Ultimately, the wind turbine serves not only as a symbol of innovative endeavor but as evidence of the perpetual human quest to capture natural curiosities for collective benefit. In understanding the mechanical conversion of wind to energy, we embrace not only sophisticated machinery but the beautiful simplicity of air meeting blade under the open sky. It is a tangible realization of potential energy—an extraordinary mechanism where the language of mechanics speaks eloquently of possibility and progress.

3.3 From Mechanical to Electrical Energy

Once upon a gusty day, the wind, having generously imparted its kinetic might to the grand blades of a wind turbine, sets the stage for an equally enchanting transformation. This dance, having premiered centuries ago with Ben Franklin flying a kite, has reached its modern-day crescendo not merely in mechanical finesse but in electrifying prowess. Transitioning from the mesmerizing whirl of turbine blades to the utilitarian hum of electric power is a feat of remarkable engineering ingenuity—one that taps into an array of scientific principles as crucial now as they were at the dawn of the electric age.

In the inner sanctum of the nacelle, where once static mechanics begin to rumble with dynamic purpose, lies the crux of electrical generation: the generator. Imagine it as the virtuoso performer within this concert, converting the vibrato of mechanical motion into the melody of electrons flowing through wires. This conversion from mechanical to electrical energy represents a monumental leap, the heart of which is elegantly captured in the choreography of magnets and coiled wires.

Let us begin with an essential question: How does mechanical spinning turn into electrical flowing? The answer, as with so many technological achievements, is rooted in the laws of physics. More specifically, the conversion leverages Faraday's law of electromagnetic induction, a principle celebrated in any physicist's toolbox. It is Michael Faraday's insight from the 19th century that gives life to this energetic ballet. The principle elegantly posits that when a conductor, such as copper wire, spirals through a magnetic field, an electrical current is excited within the conductor. Like an artist conjuring images on canvas with mere brushstrokes, the mechanical whirl spins a rotor with magnets affixed around its periphery against stationary coils of wire—the stator—thereby inducing electrical flow.

Think of the generator as a kind of sophisticated magician. As the rotor whirls ferociously at thousands of revolutions per minute, it skillfully guides magnetic fields across the stator. With each turn, electrons shuffle and spin, creating ripples of current that culminate into streams of usable electricity—an electrical equivalent of a shot of espresso: concentrated energy derived from diligent mechanical labor.

The exquisite efficacy of the generator is in its simplicity, despite the complex interactions at play. Whether a squirrel-cage induction generator or an advanced synchronous one, the underlying principle remains faithful to Faraday. Configurations might vary, yet the concept remains that of a symbiotic relationship between motion and magnetism. And in this age of carbon-cutting consciousness, the dance enters a realm where efficiency is as prized as energy production itself, with modern generators maximizing output even in fluctuating wind conditions.

Adding to this process is another element steeped in finesse: the power electronics housed alongside the generator. These devices don't just act as chaperones ensuring the energy waltz remains uninterrupted but take on the role of enthusiastic dancing partners. Through sophisticated algorithms, these electronic components stabilize the generated electricity, adjusting from the variable AC (alternating current) output of the generator to meet the grid's consistent demands, often a stable 50 or 60 Hz (hertz) frequency.

But let's not gloss over how seamlessly this conversion has integrated into our day-to-day lives. Wind turbines, in channeling their generated electricity into our homes, offices, and factories, are more visible messengers of a green revolution. They silently testify to the shift from antiquated coal plants to these modern strongholds of renewable promise. Massive energy companies and ingenious start-ups alike have recognized the elegance and efficacy of harnessing wind-based electricity generation as global electrical demand grows.

Visions of sleek, towering turbines bringing electricity to remote islands or contributing to urban grids encapsulate the democratic potential of wind energy. Imagine a rural community, illuminated for the first time by local wind farms as well as urban planners designing cities with renewables integration from step one. Governments in Europe, the Americas, and beyond embrace this futuristic turn of turbines—a tangible step toward carbon neutrality and sustainability.

In sum, the journey of mechanical energy into electrical is nothing short of exhilarating—a subtle carnival of forces, magnets, and currents collaborating with the power of natural forces. Wind turbines exemplify the commitment to clean energy—shining beacons of engineering marvel that draw upon centuries of intellectual curiosity and breakthroughs, melding old ideas with new ambitions. In them, humanity finds not just energy to power its future but a legacy of innovation, adaptation, and inspiration drawn from nature herself. The transformation from mechanical motions to electrical currents is profoundly poetic, underscoring our eternal quest to decode and harness the world's mysteries for the benefit of all.

3.4 Grid Connection and Power Distribution

As the final act in the impressive saga of wind energy conversion, the journey from the gusty whispers of the wind to the flicker of a lamp in your living room takes its last and crucial steps. In a world increasingly concerned with sustainable energy solutions, the transmission and distribution of electricity generated by wind turbines to the power grid not only underscores a commitment to clean energy but also showcases a deft harmony of technology and infrastructure.

Once the wind has played its part by spinning the colossal blades of a turbine, and the internal mechanics have worked their magic, converting kinetic energy into electricity, there remains the critical business of delivering this newfound power to the places it is needed. This is no trivial feat, and like any sophisticated logistical challenge, it requires a network of initiatives working in concert to ensure smooth delivery.

At the heart of this operation lies the electrical substation, the indispensable intermediary between wind farms and the broader power grid. Think of the substation as a sophisticated, energy-focused customs house, where power is vetted, processed, and rerouted. As electricity flows from wind turbines, it often needs its 'passport' stamped—transformed from the type suitable for internal workings (often irregular AC with variable voltages) into a more uniform output palatable to the grid. This transformation occurs thanks to transformers which adjust voltage levels, a step vital for efficient long-distance power transmission.

From the substation, electrical power embarks on its journey through transmission lines, a sprawling and unobtrusive infrastructure that weaves its way across landscapes, invisible threads of modern-day Ariadne's labyrinth. These high-voltage lines enable electricity to travel great distances with minimal loss, akin to an energy expressway. In many regions, this intricate web of wires unfolds alongside existing technological paths—railroads, roadways, and pipelines—merging human progress with natural preservation.

Here, a historical note offers perspective: the conventions underlying today's power grid were laid down in the late 19th and early 20th centuries, an era when pioneers like Thomas Edison and Nikola Tesla were sparking wars of current (AC vs. DC), each dreaming of new ways to electrify the globe. Tesla's AC system prevailed, and the major backbone of our current grid was forged, delivering electricity further and more efficiently. Fast-forward to our contemporary grid, whose continual adaptations, nevertheless, boast venerable origins.

Returning to present-day realities, distribution represents a grand finale to grid connection. After electricity has zipped along transmission lines at high voltages, it arrives near its final destinations—cities, towns, neighborhoods—with the grace of a practising gymnast poised on a beam. Here, the power faces yet another transformation. Distribution networks step in, with substations lowering voltage levels to safer, usable forms for residential and commercial consumption. This multistage transmission and distribution process ensures that by the time the electricity reaches your toaster, it's perfectly suited for your toasty requirements.

In terms of practical organization, consider microgrids and distributed generation.   While the overarching power grid is a complex beast, microgrids—self-contained, localized power systems—are enabling an exciting decentralization of power.   Within these systems, renewable energy sources, such as wind turbines, can operate autonomously, increasing resilience and independence for communities.   For example, islands with autonomous power systems can weather storms without power interruptions.

Consider too how public spaces can illustrate this symphony of supply and demand. Visualize an urban park with small wind turbines spinning artfully around the perimeter. These installations supplement the electricity needs of nearby communities, lighting pathways at night and powering Wi-Fi stations by day—a tangible reminder of renewables' integration into the fabric of daily life.

But all is not without challenge.   Integrating wind energy into the grid requires surmounting the challenge of variability—after all, the wind doesn't blow at constant speeds, and energy production can fluctuate. Intermittency is managed through technologies like energy storage systems and demand response programs that adjust consumption patterns to match energy production levels.   Ingenious solutions are in development—ranging from battery storage to innovative grid-balancing technologies—aiming to weather these fluctuations while ensuring reliability.

As wind energy's role in greening the grid expands, the conversation about grid connection embraces communities, policymakers, and engineers alike.

Decisions about infrastructure investments, regulatory requirements, and technological innovations play pivotal roles in this ongoing narrative. With an eye on efficiency and sustainability, power distribution strives to creatively integrate renewables, thus reshaping energy landscapes worldwide.

We recognize wind energy not just as a symbol of environmental hope but as an active participant within our everyday energy ethos. From the silent spin of turbines to the vibrant hum beyond our walls, this journey captures a moment in history where technology, nature, and society intertwine, orchestrating the path towards a renewable future. With each connection made, we're not just distributing power; we're empowering a vision of sustainability and innovation brighter than ever before.

3.5 Efficiency and Performance Factors

In the dynamic dance between mechanical marvel and meteorological muse, the efficiency and performance of a wind turbine play the leading roles. Much like a prima ballerina requires precise coordination and balance to captivate audiences, wind turbines must navigate an intricate set of performance factors to spin gracefully in their designated landscapes. These mighty structures, tasked with catching the wind's bounty, are judged not solely on their towering visages but on how effectively they convert a natural resource into useful energy.

First and foremost, a crucial determinant of a wind turbine's performance is the wind itself—specifically, the wind speed. Wind turbines are inherently selective creatures, performing best within specific wind speed ranges. The concept of a wind turbine's power curve illustrates this quite vividly, delineating how turbines start producing energy at a certain "cut-in" wind speed and increase output until reaching an optimal range. Past this, at exceedingly high wind speeds, performance plateaus before the "cut-out" speed stops the turbine for safety reasons.

The challenge then becomes site selection. In the vast chessboard of potential locations, the placement of a turbine is a strategically critical move. Coastal areas, open plains, and hilltops generally promise richer wind velocities, and thus more prolific energy production than valleys or areas surrounded by natural or artificial obstructions. Herein lies the historical significance of geography in wind energy. Before sophisticated modeling software, human intuition and empirically guided estimates informed siting decisions, echoing back to when ancestral methods placed windmills in drafty niches of the countryside.

Another performance consideration focuses on turbine design. Indeed, the size and shape of the blades significantly impact efficiency. Longer blades capture more wind and convert it into more energy, assuming the structure can handle the increased loads. The geometry—considering factors like pitch, twist, and taper—affects aerodynamic performance, striking a balance between lift and drag to reach a state of aerodynamic harmony.

Materials science has played a profound role in advancing turbine efficiency. Lightweight composites like fiberglass and carbon fiber enhance performance by enabling longer blades that are easier to propel with minimal wind resistance. Reducing weight reduces the energy required for rotation, leading to higher net energy gain—a delicate dance that ensures turbines are both elegant and effective in converting air into energy.

Additionally, turbine height matters. Taller turbines reach higher atmospheric layers where winds tend to be stronger and more consistent—examples of this principle are already spinning gracefully off Denmark's coast and across North America's wind belts. The quest to conquer the skies is propelled by the benefits reaped from these elevated, swirling currents.

However, innovation does not stop at basic mechanical design. Computers play a vital role, with control systems continuously fine-tuning operational parameters, such as blade pitch and yaw orientation, to balance turbine wear with performance, adapting to changing winds almost as if intuitively. This level of sophisticated control, with real-time processing, makes modern wind energy systems robust against the whims of weather—qualifying for a place in any diction of innovation.

Environmental factors too whisper in the background, influencing the symphony of performance. Weather can reflectively decide how turbines fare; ice accumulation, for example, can alter blade aerodynamics. However, ingenious techniques like heating blades from within show promise in mitigating performance drops due to ice.

Regulatory and economic influences cannot be ignored; policies that support or hinder wind projects, tax incentives, and funding play vital roles in development. A supportive stance by governments can propel the technological advancements that bolster efficiency—a concept as perennial as the wind itself, showing the power of human will to harness elemental energies.

Lastly, grid compatibility emerges as both a technical and practical aspect influencing performance. Effective grid connection, discussed previously, necessitates turbines that can adapt electricity output to grid demands. The magic lies in the harmonious blending of energy supply and consumer need, shaped by intelligent forecasting and adaptable infrastructure.

Consider, for instance, a wind farm dotting the California coastline; here, turbines harness sea breezes while mindful of marine habitats and regulatory nuances. Their blades, engineered with precision, factor material selection and aerodynamic efficiency, promising sustainable power while satisfying grid requirements.

In assessing these performance factors, we appreciate that wind turbines, much like connoisseurs of an artisanal craft, balance numerous elements to realize consistent output. The tribulations faced and overcome signal our journey from understanding basic physics to executing large-scale electrical art exhibitions seen worldwide in wind power's unmistakable profile.

The efficiency and performance of wind turbines demonstrate what happens when human creativity meets the collaborative spirit of nature, spinning dreams of a renewable future into tangible reality. Each factor, whether atmospheric or engineered, represents another thread in the magnificent tapestry of human progress and the perpetual quest to master the air.

Chapter 4

The Science of Wind

Wind is generated by atmospheric pressure differences, influenced by the Earth's rotation and uneven solar heating. It follows global patterns but also forms local phenomena. Measuring wind speed and direction provides essential data for various applications, including energy. Understanding wind's variability and climate dependence is crucial for optimizing its use in power generation and harnessing its potential effectively.

4.1   What Causes Wind

Wind, the invisible yet powerful force that plays havoc with our hair and sweeps fallen leaves into swirling dances, originates from some rather ordinarilly extraordinary processes within our atmosphere. To understand wind, we must embark on a journey of exploration through the Earth's atmospheric pressure systems, temperature variations, and a touch of the Coriolis effect, all underpinned by an ancient celestial dance powered by the Sun.

At the heart of wind creation lies a fundamental atmospheric phenomenon: pressure differences. Air pressure, the weight of the air above us, varies across the Earth's surface primarily due to unequal heating by the Sun. Imagine Earth as a planet-sized rotisserie chicken, browning unevenly under the Sun's watchful gaze. This uneven heating creates pockets of high and low pressure. Air, much like any eager concert-goer, is perpetually on the move, seeking to level out these differences by flowing from high-pressure areas to low-pressure ones. This movement is what we refer to as wind.

But how exactly does the Sun set air in motion? The process begins as solar radiation reaches the Earth's surface, warming it unevenly due to the planet's tilt and its varied topography. Areas such as the equator receive more direct sunlight, heating up quicker than regions closer to the poles. When the ground heats up, it warms the air directly above it, decreasing its density and causing it to rise. In contrast, cooler, denser air rushes in to take its place, leading to air movement and thus, the genesis of wind.

However, this straightforward explanation belies some underlying complexities. The Earth's rotation introduces a pivotal twist through the Coriolis effect. Imagine trying to draw a straight line from the North Pole to the equator while standing on a giant merry-go-round; you'd find your path curving as you move due to the spinning surface beneath your feet. Similarly, the Earth's rotation deflects the path of moving air, causing it to curve. This deflection turns straight paths into spirals–an essential factor in the formation of large-scale wind systems like trade winds and cyclones.

Global circular wind patterns, such as the Hadley Cell, further illustrate the intricate dance of the atmosphere. This large-scale circulation pattern begins at the equator, where moist, warm air ascends, creating low pressure. As it rises, it cools, moving poleward at high altitudes, and eventually descending in the subtropics as dry, cool air. This descending air causes high-pressure

54

zones, with air then moving back towards the equator, completing the cycle. These circulating cells drive the trade winds that sailors of yore depended on to navigate the world's oceans.

In essence, wind is also an unwitting participant in Earth's perpetual game of energy redistribution. Through its relentless movement, wind facilitates the transfer of heat from equatorial regions toward the poles. This balancing act is vital, moderating climates across the globe and making the planet, as we know it, livable.

While large-scale processes like those described dictate many general patterns, local factors also have their part to play. Topography can significantly alter wind patterns, creating microclimates and localized phenomena such as sea breezes. During the day, the land heats up faster than the ocean, causing the warm air over the land to rise and be replaced by cooler air from over the water. This creates a refreshing onshore breeze, ideal for flying kites on coastal afternoons. At night, the cycle reverses, with breezes flowing out to sea.

Human existence has been shaped by the whims of the wind long before we understood the science behind it. Historically, wind has been harnessed for countless endeavors–from filling the sails of ancient explorers to grinding grain in the windmills that dotted the Dutch landscape. Today, the ability to predict wind patterns fuels wind energy's ascension as a renewable power source, tapping into aeolian forces to drive turbines around the world.

Yet, as much as we continue to harness the wind to our benefit, there remains something inherently poetic about it. Perhaps it is the idea that a force stemming from such straightforward processes can wield so much power—power that has both shaped our environment and inspired our imaginations. Whether gathered on a blustery hill or watching grass sway in a gentle breeze, we stand witness to a procession of forces grander than our simple understanding—a dynamic creation story, authored by the Sun and orchestrated by the Earth, expressing itself continually across the globe.

4.2   Wind Patterns and Global Circulation

Having embarked upon the journey of understanding what causes wind, we now set sail on the broader seas of global wind patterns and atmospheric circulation. These circulating winds, like giant invisible rivers, orchestrate a complex symphony of air movements that shape not just the currents in our oceans, but also dictate weather patterns and influence climates around the world. It's a grand ballet on a planetary scale, choreographed by the Earth's rotation, redistributing heat and moisture, and unfurling its effects across every facet of life on Earth.

The Earth's atmosphere is in a state of perpetual dynamism due to the interplay of thermal gradients and the Coriolis effect, leading to the creation of several major wind belts and circulation cells. Let us, for a moment, scale back and imagine the Earth as a spinning globe, segmented into zones that each play distinct roles in the drama of global airflow. Each zone, delimited by lines of latitude, is host to its own characteristic wind systems, with the behavior of these systems imbued by the planetary forces they experience.

In the equatorial regions lies the Intertropical Convergence Zone (ITCZ), a name that may group letters awk-

wardly on the page but is crucial in the litany of wind
dynamics. Here, the fierce equatorial sun causes hot,
moist air to ascend in towering convective columns, often culminating in majestic cumulus clouds. This uproar
of ascending air leaves behind a wake of low pressure
at the surface. Previously deviously mentioned atmospheric turmoil sets the stage for the formidable trade
winds—a persistent presence whose very name evokes
the image of ancient mariners steering their ships harnessed to unseen hands of wind.

Traveling poleward, we encounter the aforementioned
Hadley Cells, and slightly further, the Ferrel Cells. The
latter demonstrates a fascinating reversal of atmospheric
roles with air flowing poleward at the surface and equa-
torward aloft. Between these cells, we find the westerlies, which prevail just as their name suggests, sweeping from the west across the temperate zones. Historically integral to the clipper ships of colonial trade routes,
these winds continue to influence today's transoceanic
journeys.

Towards the poles, the atmospheric choreography
adds another layer with the Polar Cells. Here, frigid
air descends at the poles only to travel towards the
equator at the surface, before rising once more at
around 60 degrees latitude.   While perhaps less
glamorous than their equatorial counterparts, the polar
easterlies encapsulated within these zones are no less
vital, shaping formidable cold fronts that challenge
adventurers and wildlife alike across Arctic landscapes.

To understand how these wind belts transform into
tangible patterns, one must appreciate their seamless
interaction with oceanic currents. The late 19th-century
mariner and oceanographer Matthew Fontaine Maury
first suggested that ocean currents follow major wind
patterns. His observation heralded a comprehensive

understanding of phenomena like the Gulf Stream, a warm ocean current powered by trade winds that warms the shores of western Europe, transforming Britain into more than just a location of stoic Dickensian winters.

Moreover, these widespread patterns experience seasonal adjustments, nudged afield by the tilt of the Earth's axis and the resulting shifts in solar energy distribution. During summer, for instance, the ITCZ wanders towards whichever hemisphere is basking in the sun's more direct providence, bringing rains and energizing the monsoons that drench parts of Southern Asia and Africa.

This global heritage of airflow would mean little without its significant implications for the world's climate systems. Imagine, if you will, the vacillation of the El Niño-Southern Oscillation (ENSO)—an erratic conjunction of oceanic and atmospheric phenomena passionately passed through Pacific waters. At its caprice, the pattern sweeps warm water eastwards along the equator, displacing cool upwellings, altering wind patterns, and instigating drastic climate fluctuations worldwide.

As we draw parallels from these celestial wind highways, their impact resonates profoundly with the sustained pursuit of sustainable energy. The study of global wind patterns carries far-reaching implications for the burgeoning wind-power industry. Accurately predicting wind behavior allows for optimized turbine placement and enhanced energy yields, ultimately driving us towards a cleaner, energy-abundant future. As researchers deploy sophisticated tools, such as satellite data and computational models, our understanding of these patterns continues to evolve, making wind energy one of the most dynamic fields of our times.

Even as we harness these winds to spin turbines and drive economies, there's a romance in the enduring knowledge that so much of our atmosphere's behavior, governed by forces vast and intricate, wraps the world in a concert of invisible orchestration. The patterns that emerge from this distribution reflect an interconnectedness shared by all inhabitants of this planet—one where the wafting breezes both nurture life and promise voyages beyond the horizon's reach.

4.3   Local Wind Phenomena

While the Earth's grand atmospheric circulation belts stretch across continents and oceans, the magic of wind truly reveals itself in the myriad localized phenomena that emerge from the interplay of geography, temperature, and pressure. These localized winds, distinct in character and behavior, often whisper the secrets of the terrain they traverse. Their tales, steeped in history and laced with regional idiosyncrasies, offer insights into climates that are more personal and profound.

Set the scene upon a coastal landscape, where land and sea converse through diurnal rhythms, creating wind systems that begin and end with the sun. Sea breezes offer some of the finest examples of local wind phenomena. As the day progresses, sunshine heats the land more quickly than the ocean, causing warm, light air to rise over the shore. In comes the cooler, denser air from the sea to take its place, bestowing coastal regions with refreshing gusts that have become a staple of beachside afternoons worldwide. Come night, this exchange reverses as the land cools more rapidly, setting the stage for land breezes—a quiet, often unnoticed offshore flow.

Venturing into mountainous realms, we encounter katabatic and anabatic winds, capricious companions spawned by topography. By day, when the sun's rays warm mountain slopes, the air nearest those surfaces heats up and ascends as anabatic winds. These gentle, upsloping breezes are lifelines for paragliders and hawks alike, riding thermal lifts to glide effortlessly above valleys.

By contrast, night ushers in katabatic winds—cool, dense air making its way down slopes into lowlands. Some katabatic winds gain notoriety under localized names, such as the Mistral of the Rhône Valley, which, embracing misplaced vigor, rushes toward the Mediterranean. These winds may chill vineyards but also clear skies, bathing southern France in crisp, sunny days.

In regions flanked by mountain ranges, such as the leeward sides of the Rockies or the Andes, inhabitants live under the reign of foehn winds. This warm, dry wind descends leeward slopes, having lost moisture crossing the mountains. The notorious "chinook," or "snow-eater," as it is romantically dubbed in Montana, brings dramatic warmth to winter landscapes, reducing snow cover with the rapidity of springtime revelations.

In certain parts of the world, however, local winds commandeer reputation as harbingers of hostility. The Santa Ana winds of Southern California, dry desert gusts funneled through canyons toward the coast, often portend wildfire seasons. While infamous for fuelling incendiaries, they also serve an ecological role, reshaping landscapes reliant on periodic fires for renewal.

Turning elsewhere, remote deserts face different

scenarios. Here, dust devils whirl to life, miniature tornadoes without the threat but all the spectacle. These playful dust-laden whirlwinds occur under clear skies when the surface heats rapidly, instigating spirals that dance whimsically across the arid expanse, mesmerizing and fleeting.

Local winds do more than shape climates; they shape cultures and histories, too. Across the arid lands of North Africa and the Arabian Peninsula, the sirocco marks its presence. Originating from the Sahara, this hot, gritty wind laden with dust travels north to Southern Europe, claiming mythology as its domain. Part weather event, part cultural motif, the sirocco has been blamed for everything from sleepless nights to bouts of inexplicable malaise.

Microclimates, those subtle variations on the atmospheric canvas, often take their cues from these localized winds. Picture a south-facing slope in a vineyard, where an intense sunning combined with a protective wind initiates a unique microenvironment perfect for specific grape varieties. Or consider the urban heat island effect in bustling cities, where the architectural environment coupled with anthropogenic heat creates wind patterns as distinctive as the cities themselves, ranging from pivotal breezes to heat-laden stillness.

Modern man has not only adapted to these widespread quirks of wind but has also begun to categorize them, embrace their benefits, and mitigate their harms. In renewable energy, local winds are measured conscientiously to site wind turbines optimally, harvesting energy even from areas where global patterns diminish. Urban planners now model these phenomena to guide the placement of buildings and streetscapes, creating urban designs that maximize comfort and energy efficiency.

In essence, local wind phenomena highlight nature's ever-present ingenuity. They whisper to the trees, ferry seeds across plains, and breathe life into every corner of the Earth. By becoming attuned to their presence, we become not just observers but participants in a living, breathing system of remarkable diversity and elegance. From the gentle caress of a sea breeze to the vigorous momentum of a foehn, these winds connect us to the broader rhythms of Earth's atmospheric ballet, drawing our attention ever so gently back to the sky.

4.4 Measuring Wind: Speed and Direction

If you've ever released a kite into the sky, rested beneath rustling leaves, or watched turbines spin against a clear horizon, you've encountered the enigma that is wind. Though invisible, wind is an omnipresent force, quietly influencing climates, driving ecosystems, and even powering economies. Understanding wind's essence requires more than just an observer's eye; it necessitates the meticulous measure of two core attributes: speed and direction. These have captivated and challenged humanity for generations, leading to ingenious instruments and technologies that bridge our comprehension from the simple to the sublime.

The pursuit to quantify wind's laughter and sighs commenced long ago. Ancient Greek philosopher Anaximander is often credited with developing one of the earliest known tools for observing wind, a polymath probing the mysteries of the natural world. Yet it was not until the invention of the anemometer in 1450, attributed to the prolific Italian artist Leon Battista Alberti, that a quantifiable grasp of wind speed became feasible. This device, as simple as a disc pivoting on a rod, marked the foundation upon which modern meteorology would blossom.

Fast forward a few centuries, and the anemometer has evolved but not strayed far from its ingenious roots. Today, the most common iteration marries old-world charm with new-age efficiency — behold the cup anemometer. This device typically features three or four hemispherical cups mounted on horizontal arms, revolving with the breeze. The rate at which the cups spin is directly proportional to wind speed, with modern versions employing electronic sensors to translate rotations into precise readings.

However, the symphony of tools does not end there. The sonic anemometer, a marvel of modern science, captures wind like a musician attuned to harmonic subtleties. By employing ultrasonic sound waves to measure wind velocity, these devices deftly gauge speed across three dimensions, recognizing wind's sometimes erratic dance. Sonic anemometers excel in offering precise, high-frequency data essential for fields like micrometeorology and turbulence research.

While speed captivates, the wind's direction is equally crucial. Enter the humble, yet indispensable, weather vane. Its afflicted rooster, turrets, or arrows pivot on a vertical axis, aligning with the wind. Plates located behind the rotational center catch the wind more forcefully, causing the device to align itself accordingly. Simplicity morphs into elegance, as weather vanes not only adorn rooftops but also extend their utility with digital encoders for precise readings in professional meteorological stations.

The marriage of wind measurement and technology advances further through remote sensing. Consider the lidar (Light Detection and Ranging) systems, which launch lasers to elucidate atmospheric secrets. As windborne particles reflect these laser beams back, the device calculates the wind profile at various heights, useful in modeling wind farms or understanding atmospheric dynamics.

But not all endeavours of measurement lie in gadgets and gizmos; the human touch endures. Kite anemometry, once a niche but now revitalized for large-scale applications, measures wind by tracking the flight dynamics of tethered kites. This reactive, yet robust, approach unfolds across expanses where traditional apparatuses falter, breathing life into aerial exploration for renewable energy maximization.

Now, as we draw closer to the whisper of the elements, raw data transmutes into practical application. Consider aviation, where grasping wind speed and direction from various altitudes ensures safety in the skies. Pilots strategically use tailwinds to expedite journeys and negotiate headwinds with calculated precision, informed by data from wind profilers scanning altitudes up to 15 kilometers above the Earth's surface.

In agriculture, wind measurement optimizes yield and sustainability. Farmers, wise to the whims of the wind, plant shelterbelts and construct windbreaks based on analyzed patterns, promoting microclimates conducive to productivity. Urban planners similarly exploit wind data to design cities that harness natural ventilation while safeguarding against gusty gales.

The frontier of wind measurement holds promise in addressing ever-pressing climate challenges. By tapping into high-altitude winds, exploration ventures such as the Stratospheric Controlled Perturbation Experiment (SCoPEx) investigate geoengineering possibilities. Unraveling the potential of upper atmospheric winds could offer new perspectives on energy transfer and climate intervention.

As we wrap ourselves in the garments of history and science, our pursuit to understand wind through measurement bridges the ephemeral with the tangible. By exploring dimensions of speed and direction, our instruments, simple and complex, enlighten us more than ever before. Through time-honored intuition and cutting-edge science, our picture of these invisible currents becomes less a mystery and more a masterpiece of atmospheric alchemy. So next time the wind whispers secrets between the leaves, consider the joint labor of ancient thinkers and modern innovators who have long labored to grant us the power to listen.

4.5 Wind Climate and Variability

From the gentle caress of a summer breeze to the fierce howl of a winter storm, wind reveals its multifaceted nature through an intricate tapestry of variability. This variability, manifesting across temporal and spatial scales, plays a crucial role in defining local climates and serving as a pivot point for the burgeoning wind energy sector. Understanding these shifts and patterns demands a keen eye, an open mind, and an appreciation for the dynamic dance of atmospheric forces.

Wind exists as part of an ever-evolving climate system, a system that envelops the Earth with its complexity and occasional whimsy. To understand wind climate is to delve into a realm where global patterns interweave with local circumstances, painting a picture that's both pre-dictable and chaotic. On this vast stage, the cast of characters includes everything from the rhythmic seasonal monsoons to the erratic pulses of storm fronts.

Let us consider the intricate play of seasons, a prime example of wind variability over time. Seasonal winds, such as the monsoons, illustrate how climatic cycles are inherently linked to temperature contrasts between land and sea. In India, the monsoon rains that sweep across the subcontinent from June to September are driven by the dramatic seasonal reversal of wind patterns. This reversal is so significant that it defines the agricultural calendar and the cultural fabric for millions.

But wind's temperament is not solely subject to seasonal whims. On shorter timescales, phenomena such as cyclones can deliver sudden and impactful changes in wind conditions. These powerful systems not only alter local climates temporarily but also provide a stark illustration of the raw, unbridled force of nature's breath. While cyclones are a bane to human infrastructure, they are crucial to the redistribution of oceanic heat, significantly influencing global climate patterns.

As we shift our lens to a broader view, the global wind belts, like the trade winds and westerlies, also play a defining role in regional climates. These persistent winds have steered exploration in both ancient and modern times, while also sculpting landscapes through the steady, patient work of natural erosion.

Within this grand orchestration, there exists a crucial technological interface—wind energy. The challenge for wind energy lies in navigating the tempest of variability, transforming it from an obstacle into an asset. In nature's spontaneity lies a wealth of potential. Wind turbines, standing sentinel across windswept plains and rugged coasts, are designed not unlike musical instruments, tuned to the symphony of invisible air currents.

The efficiency of wind farms hinges on a deep understanding of wind characterization over different timescales—ranging from instantaneous gusts to enduring seasonal shifts. Meteorologists and engineers collaborate to harness data, weaving complex models that predict wind behavior, helping them identify optimal turbine locations that promise the most consistent energy output.

Spatial variability, guided by geographical features, is another cornerstone of the wind climate. From the steppes of Central Asia to the blustery channels of Patagonia, topography molds wind's character, dictating its course and intensity. Mountain ranges redirect and intensify winds, fostering microclimates that shape the local environment and its inhabitants. On coastal areas, weaving a story rich with history and future promise, the interplay between land and sea encourages the thriving of offshore wind farms, poised to become titans of sustainable energy production.

However, like any tale, this narrative is not without its foreboding. Climate change, the great disruptor, whispers uncertainty into the patterns and paths of wind. As global temperatures rise, atmospheric circulation begins to shift, threatening to rewrite climate norms that have existed for millennia. For the wind energy sector, this presents both challenge and opportunity. The industry must remain adaptive, developing technologies not just for capturing energy, but for anticipating metamorphoses in wind patterns that may emerge as the Earth continues warming.

In navigating these challenges, innovation becomes the wind industry's compass. Engineers and scientists are now leveraging advances such as artificial intelligence to derive insights from data previously considered too chaotic or complex. Through simulations that predict future wind scenarios, the industry stands better prepared to deploy resources strategically and maintain energy reliability even amidst climatic flux.

Ultimately, the study of wind climate and variability entwines us in a narrative of interdependence between nature and humanity. As we seek to harness the wind for energy, we are not merely tapping into a renewable resource, but engaging with an elemental force that has shaped our planet's climate and, by extension, our very existence. Each gust of wind carries not just the power of motion but also the accumulated knowledge of centuries—its ebb and flow foretells stories of a changing world. As we move onward, it is with a sense of curiosity and stewardship that we embrace the paradox of variability, transforming what once seemed capricious into a symphony harmonious with the planet's aspirations for a sustainable future.

Chapter 5

Types of Wind Turbines

Wind turbines are primarily categorized into horizontal and vertical axis designs, each with distinct operational advantages. Small and micro turbines serve localized energy needs, while offshore variants exploit maritime winds. Emerging technologies introduce innovative designs that enhance efficiency and adaptability. Understanding these diverse types is key to selecting the appropriate turbine for specific energy demands and environmental conditions.

5.1   Horizontal Axis Wind Turbines

When one pictures a wind turbine, the quintessential image that springs to mind is likely a Horizontal Axis Wind Turbine (HAWT). These graceful giants, with their iconic trio of elongated blades sweeping through the skies, have become the face of modern wind energy. Dominating the landscape of renewable power, HAWTs are not just the most common type of wind turbine; they are central to the ongoing transition towards sustainable energy systems across the globe. In this section, we unravel the nuances and explore the distinctive features, historical evolution, and the operational prowess of horizontal axis wind turbines.

To appreciate the prevalence of HAWTs, one must first understand their fundamental design. These turbines have a rotor shaft positioned horizontally, akin to the axis of a spinning top, aligned with the wind's direction. As the wind flows over the blades, it generates lift—much like an airplane wing—causing the rotor to spin. This rotation drives a generator, transforming kinetic energy into electricity. Simple in concept yet intricate in design, HAWTs embody a synergy of physics, engineering, and environmental science.

The origins of HAWTs can be traced back centuries, long before electricity became a household necessity. In medieval Europe, these windmills were instrumental in grinding grain and pumping water. The quintessential Dutch windmills are classic early examples of horizontal axis designs, though they were far removed from the sleek, efficient machines we see today. As technology progressed, so too did the applications and efficiency of wind turbines. By the late 19th century, the movement to convert wind into electricity began, marking a pivotal moment in industrial history.

Modern HAWTs can vary tremendously in size, ranging from modest 1 kilowatt units used for residential power to massive 8 megawatt giants gracing offshore installations. Their design has been meticulously refined over the years to maximize efficiency, even in the face of fluctuating wind speeds. They are often lauded for their high efficiency rather than simple appearance. This efficiency primarily stems from their ability to achieve higher tip speeds, maximizing energy capture from the wind.

A critical component of this efficiency is the aerodynamic design of the blades. Crafted from lightweight but robust materials like fiberglass or carbon fiber, each blade is carefully shaped to optimize lift-to-drag

70

ratios. The longer the blades, the greater the swept area, and thus, the more energy can be harvested. However, longer blades also require more robust support structures and precise engineering to prevent catastrophic failures.

Beyond the blades, another vital mechanism of HAWTs is their yaw control system. This ingenious technology allows the nacelle—the housing atop the turbine tower— to rotate and face the wind directly. By utilizing sensors, computer systems, and motors, the yaw system ensures that wind energy is captured most effectively, irrespective of changing wind directions. This adaptability to variable conditions is a testament to the sophisticated nature of modern HAWT technologies.

The towering presence of HAWTs across landscapes worldwide is no coincidence; their positioning is a strategic fusion of geography and engineering. Developers often embark on extensive studies before selecting locations, balancing factors such as wind speed, direction, and environmental impact. Onshore installations, commonly found in plains or hilly regions, capitalize on consistent terrestrial winds. In contrast, offshore HAWTs harness the unrestricted and generally stronger winds found at sea, albeit with added technical challenges related to marine environments.

While HAWTs command prominence, they are not without their challenges. Critics often cite their visual and noise impacts, perceived as intrusive by some communities. There is also the issue of intermittency—the wind doesn't always blow when electricity is needed, necessitating the integration of storage solutions or complementary energy sources. Nonetheless, advancements in turbine technology, grid integration, and energy storage are continually mitigating these issues, paving the way for enhanced adoption.

The public perception and policy crucially influence the deployment of HAWTs. Governments worldwide encourage their adoption through incentives and regulations aimed at fostering renewable energy growth. The push towards decarbonization, amidst growing climate concerns, has further expanded the footprint of HAWTs—literally and figuratively—into national energy strategies.

Horizontal axis wind turbines stand as pillars of modern renewable energy infrastructure, embodying innovation, adaptability, and ecological consciousness. As technological advancements forge ahead, they promise to deliver even greater efficiencies and broader applications. By understanding the mechanics, history, and future potential of HAWTs, we gain a deeper appreciation for these marvels of modern engineering, which are quietly yet powerfully transforming our energy landscapes.

5.2 Vertical Axis Wind Turbines

In the diverse world of wind turbines, one might imagine all to be towering, three-bladed giants like their horizontal axis counterparts. However, lurking in the corners of this evolving technology is a less conspicuous yet equally intriguing alternative: the Vertical Axis Wind Turbine (VAWT). Though they might appear to be the underdogs in the wind energy arena, VAWTs bring their unique set of advantages to the table, challenging the conventional wind power paradigm.

A vertical axis wind turbine is essentially a turbine where the rotor shaft stands perpendicular to the ground and vertical in relation to the wind flow. The unusual design allows VAWTs to harness wind energy irrespective of wind direction. Their structures often resemble futuristic sculptures more than traditional turbines, adding an aesthetic flair to function.

Historically, VAWTs are not a novel concept. The genesis of vertical axis wind turbine technology can be traced back to Persian windmills of the 7th to 9th centuries, characterized by their vertical sails built of bundled reeds or wood. These ancient machines fueled agricultural and industrial activities long before the concept of electricity generation even existed. The re-emergence of VAWTs in modern contexts owes much to their potential as convenient alternatives, especially in urban environments where space and wind directions pose challenges.

The defining distinctions of VAWTs from their horizontal relatives are more than just geometric. Perhaps the most pronounced advantage of VAWTs is their omnidirectional capability. Since the rotor can capture wind from any direction without the need for yaw control mechanisms, they offer significant simplification in design and operation. This quality makes them particularly suitable for locations where the wind shifts frequently, such as urban areas or complex terrains.

VAWTs are often lauded for their lower starting torque. Thanks to their structural configuration, they can potentially operate at lower wind speeds where horizontal turbines might remain idle. This aspect can prove advantageous in regions where wind conditions are less consistently robust, enabling alternative energy capture even when the breeze is just a whisper.

One cannot discuss VAWTs without addressing their suitability for urban environments. Unlike their horizontal axis counterparts, which require clear, open landscapes to maximize energy capture, VAWTs can stand adaptedly between skyscrapers or beside highways, where intermittent wind tunnels are more the rule than the exception.   Their operation, also generally quieter, mitigates noise pollution concerns, further advocating their place within the urban tapestry.

A particularly innovative form of the VAWT is the Darrieus model, the brainchild of French engineer Georges Darrieus in the 1920s.   Characterized by its eggbeater shape, the Darrieus turbine is a scientific spectacle, leveraging aerodynamics to produce lift efficiently.   While aesthetically captivating, it does present challenges in stability and requires meticulous engineering to maintain operational integrity.

Equally impressive is the Savonius turbine, which embraces a simpler, lower-profile design featuring scooped blades reminiscent of a classical anemometer. Though less efficient in wind-to-electricity conversion, its rugged simplicity and ease of construction—often predominately metal or heavy plastic—make it ideal for small-scale, personal use or auxiliary power. The Savonius's spinning silhouette is a testament to how traditional concepts can be repurposed with contemporary expertise.

Despite their advantages, VAWTs face notable challenges in efficiency and energy output compared to the more predominant HAWTs. The design's inherent limitation lies in the blades often passing through slower-moving air, resulting in a performance dropout as the blade rotates through its cycle.   Moreover, the mechanical stresses involved call for robust and sometimes costly structural materials to ensure durability.

In the race for renewable solutions, the future of VAWTs is buoyed by ongoing research and technological advances aiming to optimize their efficiency and cost-effectiveness. Scientists and engineers are relentlessly pursuing improvements in blade design, materials, and energy storage integration to overcome existing efficiency deficits and maximize the potential of VAWTs.

As wind energy continues to attract investment worldwide, particularly with increasing emphasis on low carbon footprints and renewable portfolios, VAWTs are carving their niche. Their adaptability, lower environmental impact, and potential for aesthetic integration make them attractive prospects, especially as urban centers seek sustainable energy solutions amidst skyscraper jungles.

Vertical Axis Wind Turbines stand as a symbol of resilience and innovation within the eclectic collection of wind energy technologies. Their journey from ancient mechanisms to cutting-edge urban applications epitomizes the blend of historical wisdom and contemporary design in renewable energy paradigms. While they may not have ascended to the same iconic status as their horizontal cousins, their ability to thrive where others falter continuously reinvigorates their role on the global energy stage. Amidst the winds of change, VAWTs serve as a reminder that in the art of harnessing nature, sometimes thinking differently is precisely what propels us forward.

5.3 Small and Micro Wind Turbines

As the conversation around renewable energy grows ever more urgent, the concept of harnessing the wind has trickled from grandiose utility-scale installations to more personal domains. Enter the realm of small and micro wind turbines, where the world of renewable energy gets up close and personal, scaling down wind power to suit individual needs and smaller communities. These diminutive yet mighty machines promise to democratize green energy, offering sustainable power solutions outside the confines of sprawling wind farms.

Small and micro wind turbines differ primarily in scale and intended use from their larger brethren. Whereas large turbines are typically geared toward generation on a commercial scale, supplying vast quantities of energy to the grid, small and micro turbines carve out a niche in the world of residential, agricultural, and localized power solutions. These turbines excel at bringing the benefits of wind power directly to the consumer, whether perched on the roof of a home, settled next to a barn, or standing in a small field, working steadily to reduce the user's carbon footprint.

To understand the appeal of these smaller turbines, it is essential first to demystify their purpose and potential. Typically, small wind turbines refer to systems with capacities ranging from 1 kilowatt up to 100 kilowatts, while micro turbines clock in at substantially lower output levels, usually under 1 kilowatt. Despite their reduced size, these turbines can significantly impact local energy needs, particularly where traditional electrical infrastructure is lacking or renewable inclination is high.

One of the most compelling advantages of small and micro wind turbines is their ability to empower individual users with energy independence. Homeowners blessed with consistent winds can leverage this natural resource to lessen reliance on traditional energy sources. These turbines are not just a boon to isolated regions devoid of grid access but can serve urban settings where ecological considerations or energy sovereignty are top priorities.

The appeal here lies also in customization. Small and

micro turbines can be specially tailored to fit the specifics of the given environment they inhabit. Specific models are designed to accommodate lower wind speeds, making them viable in areas where larger turbines might struggle. The flexibility extends beyond technical specifications to installation locales—on rooftops, stand-alone poles, or even in off-grid situations where they can supplement other renewables like solar panels.

On the technological frontier, the evolution of small and micro turbines mirrors trends seen in other renewable technologies, benefiting from advances in materials science, efficiency, and engineering know-how. Innovations such as helical blade designs and direct-drive systems are leading to more efficient and quieter turbines, overcoming some of the traditional objections related to noise and maintenance demands.

An undeniable attraction of these compact turbines is their role as educational tools. They provide a tangible entry point into the world of renewable energy for individuals and institutions. Schools, for example, utilize micro wind turbines to teach students about clean energy, sustainability, and engineering principles. Their installation doesn't just generate power; it creates opportunities for knowledge power, instilling values of environmental stewardship in future generations.

From a historical perspective, the modern small and micro wind turbine takes its cue from earlier grassroots energy movements. The 1970s energy crises seeded interest in alternative energy and personal power systems. Enthusiasts and environmental pioneers experimented with homemade turbines, sowing the seeds for today's more refined, market-ready products. These early adopters were driven as much by ideology as energy needs, establishing the blueprint for the subsequent development of small-scale wind systems.

The proliferation of small and micro wind turbines faces some hurdles, predominantly centered around zoning regulations, aesthetic objections, and wind availability.   Authorities in various jurisdictions may place restrictions on their installation due to concerns about noise, visual impact, and structural safety.   Moreover, not every location may provide the sustained wind speeds necessary for effective operation, underscoring the importance of thorough site assessments before installation.

Practically, small and micro turbines can find diverse applications. In rural setups, they can power agricultural equipment, reducing fuel costs and reliance on conventional electricity. For the outdoor enthusiast owning a remote cabin, a micro wind turbine might light up the gloomy evening with energy to spare for electronic gadgets. In urban environments keen on renewable integration, small turbines might supplement solar installations, offering a hybrid approach to residential energy needs.

Small and micro wind turbines exemplify how renewable energy technology can be scaled to meet the individual's exigent needs. Their ability to generate clean energy, customized fitting to the whims of wind conditions and locales, paired with technological advancements, makes them an exciting option for energy-conscious individuals and communities. These turbines present a vision of an energy future where the power of the wind is not just a resource harvested by distant giants but a prevalent force charting personal pathways toward sustainability. As the world continues to grapple with the imperatives of climate change, even a small turbine in the backyard could make a difference in bridging present hopes with future realities.

5.4 Offshore Wind Turbines

In a world increasingly focused on sustainable solutions, the quest for renewable energy often leads us to the open sea. Here, away from bustling cities and sprawling landscapes, offshore wind turbines rise from the waves, punctuating the horizon like giant sailors harnessing the ceaseless winds. These turbines are a testament to human ingenuity, a bold embrace of nature's most potent forces, echoing the age-old relationship between mankind and the sea.

Offshore wind farms represent a natural evolution of wind energy technology, moving from land-based installations to larger, more ambitious projects located on water. These turbines are anchored to the seabed in relatively shallow seas, typically no more than 60 meters deep, though technological advances are pushing these limits further into the open ocean. The allure of offshore locations is multifaceted, driven by the promise of stronger, more consistent winds compared to their onshore counterparts.

The advantages of offshore wind turbines begin with these wind patterns. Over the open water, winds are generally stronger and less turbulent than over land. This reliability allows turbines to operate at a higher capacity, generating more energy and thus making them an attractive option for countries aiming to meet renewable energy targets. Moreover, offshore wind farms can be located near coastal populations, which are often densely populated and demand significant amounts of electricity. This proximity reduces transmission distances and potential energy loss, making offshore installations a strategically advantageous component of national energy grids.

From a historical perspective, offshore wind development is a relatively recent innovation. The first offshore wind farm, Vindeby, was constructed off the coast of Denmark in 1991. This pioneering endeavor laid the groundwork for subsequent projects by demonstrating technical feasibility and economic viability. Since then, countries like the United Kingdom, Germany, and China have embraced offshore wind as a cornerstone of their renewable energy strategies, investing heavily in developing technology and infrastructure.

However, the underwater frontier is not devoid of its challenges. The engineering feats required to establish and maintain offshore turbines are nothing short of Herculean. Turbines must withstand the assault of saltwater corrosion, hostile weather conditions, and the complex dynamics of marine ecosystems. Maintenance operations, already a significant consideration on land, become exponentially more challenging at sea, necessitating specialized vessels and crews to perform even routine repairs.

Then there's the cost. Offshore turbines are significantly more expensive to install and maintain than their terrestrial counterparts, primarily due to the complexities of marine construction and logistics. However, economies of scale and technological advancements are driving costs down. Turbine manufacturers are producing larger, more efficient machines capable of generating unprecedented amounts of energy, promising to tip the cost-benefit balance in favor of broader adoption.

Environmental considerations also take center stage when discussing offshore wind facilities. While the visual impact might be reduced compared to onshore installations—since they are often far from the naked eye—there are ecological impacts to consider. The construction and operation of wind farms can affect marine life, from the seabed habitats disturbed during installation to the avian and aquatic creatures that might interact with the turbines themselves. However, research indicates that with careful planning and mitigation strategies, these impacts can be minimized. Moreover, some studies suggest offshore turbines might even create artificial reefs, contributing positively to marine biodiversity.

Real-world projects exemplify the potential of offshore wind. The Hornsea Project in the UK proudly holds the title of the largest offshore wind farm globally. Upon completion, it is expected to power over one million homes. In the United States, projects like Vineyard Wind are set to launch, heralding the country's foray into large-scale offshore wind energy. Such projects highlight the growing confidence and capability in this area, backed by robust policy support and substantial financial commitment.

In examining offshore wind energy, we also delve into a broader narrative about the transition to renewables. As land and resources become scarcer, the ocean offers a seemingly limitless expanse with untapped potential. Offshore wind is central to this broader strategy, enabling countries to increase their renewable portfolios and meet ambitious emissions reduction targets.

Offshore wind turbines represent a fusion of engineering prowess and ecological aspiration. They've transformed the open seas from solitary stretches into bustling hubs of innovation and sustainability. As technology continues to advance, decreasing costs and mitigating environmental impacts, offshore wind stands as a beacon of hope in the global shift towards cleaner energy. Silent sentinels over the ocean's expanse, these turbines remind us of renewable energy's capacity to harness nature not just for sustenance, but for sustainable progress.

5.5   Innovative Designs and Technologies

As the winds of change sweep across the landscape of renewable energy, we're entering an era marked by exciting innovations in wind turbine design and technology. These advancements promise not only to redefine our energy infrastructure but also to push the boundaries of what wind energy can achieve. In a world desperately seeking sustainable solutions, these emerging technologies stand as harbingers of a greener tomorrow.

Wind energy has seen remarkable growth, with familiar, large-scale turbines dominating the plains and seas. However, meeting future energy demands and environmental targets calls for more than just expansion—it calls for evolution. This evolution comes through innovative designs that address the limitations of traditional turbines. These designs are diverse, ranging from improvements in efficiency and adaptability to novel concepts that challenge our fundamental understanding of harnessing the wind.

One of the most revolutionary concepts catching the wind is bladeless turbine technology. This design defies convention by eschewing blades altogether. Instead, it relies on the principle of vortex-induced vibration to generate power. As wind flows past the turbine's cylindrical structure, it induces oscillations. These vibrations are converted into energy, offering a solution that's quieter, less harmful to wildlife, and boasts a lower visual impact. Though still in developmental stages, prototypes like the Vortex Bladeless wind turbine demonstrate an exciting frontier in energy capture.

Alongside bladeless designs, modular systems are gaining attention. Wind turbines traditionally consist of monolithic structures requiring significant logistical challenges for transport and assembly. In contrast, modular wind turbines are built from multiple, smaller components that are easier to manufacture and assemble on-site. This innovation not only reduces installation costs but also opens doors for deployment in difficult-to-reach locations, potentially unlocking new wind resources previously deemed inaccessible.

Moving into the skies, airborne wind energy systems (AWES) present another visionary leap. These systems use tethered devices, such as kites or drones, to capture wind energy at higher altitudes—up to several kilometers above ground. Here, winds are generally stronger and more consistent. By accessing this high-altitude wind, AWES can generate energy with potentially greater efficiency than ground-based systems. The Makani Energy Kite, acquired by Google, exemplifies this approach by flying in a circular path while tethered to a ground station, creating energy through on-board turbines.

The ocean itself is not merely a site for offshore fixed-foundation turbines but a place for exploration via floating wind technology. Floating wind turbines are anchored with mooring systems in deep waters where traditional foundations are impractical. These floating structures can be installed in regions with abundant wind resources that can't support fixed turbines. Hywind Scotland, the first floating wind farm, has shown that this technology can operate successfully and promises to drive down costs as it matures.

Intertwined with these architectural innovations are technological advancements improving efficiency and monitoring. Smart sensors and data analytics now play a critical role in turbine operations. These technologies allow real-time monitoring and predictive maintenance, minimizing downtime and optimizing performance. By integrating machine learning and big data, operators can anticipate faults and schedule maintenance proactively, thus reducing costs and enhancing reliability.

Explorations into material science have also borne fruit, promising stronger, lighter turbines. Carbon fiber and other composite materials are increasingly applied to manufacture blades. These materials can extend the lifespan and performance of turbines while reducing the weight burden on the structure. Additionally, bio-materials offer an environmentally friendly aspect, with ongoing research into biodegradable and recyclable wind turbine components minimizing the lifecycle environmental impact.

On the energy integration side, innovative storage solutions are being developed to address the intermittency of wind power. Advances in battery technology, hydrogen storage, and virtual power plants aim to harness the variability of the wind. By smoothing out supply and demand fluctuations, these technologies provide stable energy delivery to the grid and enhance the overall viability of wind power.

Looking toward the horizon, visionary concepts fuel our imagination. Biomimicry, the practice of drawing design inspiration from nature, is inspiring new turbine shapes and configurations. Designs emulating the motion of whales' fins or schools of fish may improve efficiency by utilizing natural fluid dynamics principles. These bio-inspired turbines strive for harmony with nature, likely leading to reduced environmental impact and improved performance in diverse conditions.

The future of wind energy is as boundless as the creative spirit driving it. By capturing the power of the wind in inventive new ways, these innovative designs and technologies echo our collective aspiration toward sustainable growth and a commitment to writing a sustainable narrative for generations to come.

Chapter 6

The Benefits of Wind Energy

Wind energy offers environmental benefits by reducing carbon emissions and reliance on fossil fuels. Economically, it drives job creation and stimulates growth in the energy sector. Its renewable nature enhances energy security and independence. Additionally, wind projects can promote local community development and infrastructure improvements. These advantages underscore its pivotal role in fostering a sustainable and resilient energy future.

6.1   Environmental Advantages

In recent years, amid an intensifying climate crisis, the discourse around renewable energies has gained unprecedented momentum. Central to these discussions is wind energy, lauded not only for its technological charm—spinning turbines gracefully orchestrating the conversion of wind's kinetic energy into electricity—but also for its profound environmental advantages. A notable pillar in combating climate change, wind energy plays a crucial role in reducing carbon emissions and fostering a more sustainable future.

At the heart of this discussion lies a compelling metric: carbon dioxide (CO_2) emissions, the primary driver of global warming. The burning of fossil fuels for energy production releases vast quantities of CO_2, exacerbating the greenhouse effect and leading to global temperature rise. In stark contrast, wind energy stands tall as a zero-emission powerhouse during operation, offering an elegant solution by harnessing an inexhaustible natural resource.

The environmental advantages of wind energy first gained tangible traction in the 1970s during the oil crisis, as societies around the world started to recognize the vulnerability of heavy reliance on fossil fuels. Early adopters, particularly in Europe and the United States, initiated a paradigm shift towards renewable energy sources, laying the groundwork for the wind industry as we know it today. The motivation was obvious: reduce dependency on finite resources, alleviate environmental degradation, and pursue cleaner, more sustainable alternatives.

Wind energy significantly contributes to carbon footprint reduction. Estimates suggest that for every megawatt hour (MWh) of electricity generated via wind instead of fossil-based sources, approximately 0.5 to 1 ton of CO_2 emissions can be avoided. This impact becomes evident when considering that a single large wind turbine can generate enough electricity annually to offset the emissions equivalent to that produced by hundreds of cars.

But the story of wind energy's environmental benefits extends beyond mere numbers. It thrives in the midst of an ecological narrative that champions biodiversity and clean air. Unlike coal-fired or natural gas power plants, wind energy operations do not emit air pollutants such as sulfur dioxide or nitrogen oxides, which are notorious for non-carbon polluting effects. These pollutants can lead to acid rain, smog, and detrimental health effects in humans, impacting respiratory systems.

An exemplary illustration of wind energy's environmental stewardship can be observed in Denmark, a veritable pioneer in integrating wind power. Currently, over 40% of Denmark's electricity demand is met by wind energy, setting a robust precedent for other nations eager to transition to renewables. This shift not only demonstrates a significant reduction in emissions but also symbolizes a commitment to an environmentally conscious trajectory that supports both local communities and global ecosystems.

Delving further into the landscape of climate change mitigation, wind energy's benefits are amplified when juxtaposed with the environmental footprint of alternative energy sources. While the production and installation of wind turbines do require materials and energy—resulting in some initial emissions—these are overwhelmingly compensated by the emissions saved during their operational lifespan. The energy payback time for a wind turbine is generally less than a year, meaning the emissions reduction kicks in early and persists long after the initial investment in resources has been recuperated.

Critics may point to the aesthetic and acoustic implications of wind installations, as well as their impact on avian life, as environmental concerns. However, technological advancements, strategic siting, and rigorous environmental assessments have greatly mitigated these issues. Modern turbines are designed to be quieter and more efficient, and bird-friendly initiatives are increasingly being implemented to minimize wildlife disruption. These adaptations showcase an industry responsive to ecological considerations, continually evolving to harmonize human needs with natural coherence.

The environmental advantages of wind energy extend beyond national borders, cementing its role in collective global efforts.   International agreements, such as the Paris Agreement, underscore the necessity for renewables in national energy mixes.   Countries are working towards ambitious targets to cap global temperature increases, with wind energy poised as a central figure in reaching these milestones by complementing other renewables to decarbonize the energy grid.

The journey towards a low-carbon future is full of challenges, yet the promise of wind energy invites a cleaner, sustainable horizon.   It embodies the convergence of technological sophistication and ecological mindfulness, advocating a legacy that future generations may one day view not merely as an alternative, but as the norm.   As nations continue their quest for sustainable innovations, embracing wind energy's potential could very well instigate a transformative leap, propelling humanity toward a prosperous, carbon-neutral era.

The environmental advantages of wind energy are as formidable as the gentle yet persistent breath of the winds themselves.   In the grand tapestry of climate action, wind energy offers an integral thread that weaves environmental stewardship into the heart of human progress.   It invites societies to embrace a sustainable ethos, ensuring that the air we breathe is cleaner, the planet we inhabit is healthier, and the legacy we leave is one of stewardship and foresight.

6.2 Economic Impact and Job Creation

As we journey through the expansive field of renewable energy, the economic tapestry wrought by the wind industry emerges as both dynamic and transformative. Beyond its environmental accolades, wind energy stands as a robust catalyst for economic growth and job creation, spinning opportunities as readily as it does its mighty blades.

The wind energy sector's impact on the economy is multifaceted, rippling outwards to touch local, national, and global financial landscapes. It offers a unique proposition: harnessing a naturally occurring, cost-free resource—wind—to generate economic value, which naturally attracts interest from investors, governments, and communities alike.

Historically, the ascent of wind energy has been marked by substantial investment, fueled by the increasing disparity between finite fossil resources and ever-growing energy demands. This shift has precipitated a wave of economic activity. To grasp the full extent of wind energy's economic prowess, we must delve into its direct and indirect contributions to job creation.

Direct employment within the wind industry spans a broad array of roles. From the conception and design of technology to engineering, project development, manufacturing, and maintenance, the industry supports a diverse workforce. Each wind project requires meticulous planning, skilled manufacturing of components, methodical transportation logistics, and precise installation—resulting in a steady demand for jobs across various skill levels.

Consider the manufacturing of wind turbine components. Producing towers, blades, generators, and other

91

essential parts demands not only technical expertise but also a scalable workforce. Regions with an established manufacturing base, such as parts of Europe and North America, have notably benefited as factories proliferate, breathing life into local economies. The intricate supply chain attracts both large and small enterprises, encouraging regional economic diversification and resilience.

In addition to direct employment, the wind sector spawns a host of indirect jobs. As wind farms burgeon, the demand for raw materials escalates, strengthening businesses in sectors like steel production and electronic components. Moreover, secondary services—ranging from transport and logistics to legal, environmental, and financial services—become integral to the industry's ecosystem, collectively reinforcing economic growth through their symbiotic relationship with wind power projects.

On a more localized level, the influx of wind energy projects can revitalize rural and economically marginalized areas. Traditionally, these regions have hosted industrial operations tied to fossil resources, which are waning. Enter wind energy— a rejuvenating force, offering a sustainable development strategy by securing long-term contracts for land use, which translate into stable income for landowners. Communities witness improved infrastructure, from road enhancements to new service facilities, resulting from these investments.

Globally, the wind sector is recognized as a crucial player in fostering economic development. Aligning with international commitments to sustainable energy, countries are increasingly adopting wind technologies, catalyzing competitive advantage in the global market while fostering energy independence. Policies and incentives introduced by governments to support the renewable transition further stimulate economic activity, drawing in private sector investment.

A particularly illustrative example can be found in Germany's "Energiewende" (energy transition) initiative. By setting ambitious targets for renewable energy generation, Germany has successfully mobilized its economy around clean energy, turning wind power into a cornerstone of both its energy policy and economic strategy. The result? Thousands of jobs created, cementing Germany as a leader in wind technology and an exemplar to the world.

The economic vitality engendered by wind energy is underpinned by cost dynamics. Recent years have witnessed a remarkable decline in the cost of wind-generated electricity, thanks to technological advancements and economies of scale. As such, wind energy is rapidly becoming one of the most economically feasible sources of new power generation. This cost competitiveness fuels further investment, job creation, and economic interconnection as wind projects become more widely adopted.

However, transforming wind's economic prospects into tangible, widespread benefits requires navigating challenges such as fluctuating market conditions, policy uncertainties, and technological hurdles. To harness wind's full potential, investment in education and training is paramount, ensuring a workforce that evolves in step with the industry's technological advancements and increasing complexity.

As the sun sets on traditional energy paradigms and rises on innovative, sustainable alternatives, wind energy stands at the forefront—a stalwart industry both tethered to and liberated by the gales of change. Its capacity to foster economic growth and job creation renders it an invaluable player in current and aspiring economies alike.

The wind energy sector epitomizes economic promise: a confluence of sustainable resource management with dynamic job creation that champions innovation and resilience. By propelling economic growth and sowing the seeds of myriad employment opportunities, wind energy reinforces the notion that ecological sensitivity and economic robustness are not only compatible but indeed symbiotic pursuits. As the world collectively harnesses the winds of progress, the promise of wind energy beckons a future where prosperity and sustainability are inextricably linked.

6.3   Energy Independence and Security

In a world where geopolitical tensions and fluctuating fossil fuel markets can send shockwaves through global economies, the quest for energy independence and security has never been more relevant. Amidst this backdrop, wind energy emerges not just as an environmental savior or economic catalyst, but as a linchpin in the pursuit of energy sovereignty, reducing the strings that fossil fuel reliance holds over nations.

For centuries, countries have been tethered to fossil fuels, not just as a primary energy source, but as commodities that wield economic and political power. The control of oil and gas reserves has often dictated, perhaps even manipulated, international relations and policy decisions— an enigma unwoven by the promise of renewables. However, wind energy represents a paradigm shift, offering the potential to decentralize power and fortify a nation's control over its energy resources.

The historical arc of energy security is illustrated by relentless cycles of dependency and crisis. Consider the oil embargoes of the 1970s, which exposed the vulnerability of countries heavily reliant on imported oil. These events marked a turning point and kindled an interest in diversifying energy portfolios—a nascent recognition of the strategic importance of renewables.

Fast forward to today, and wind energy's role in enhancing energy independence is increasingly evident. The capacity to generate electricity from domestic wind resources diminishes the need for imports, essentially allowing countries to wean themselves off the volatile fossil fuel chain. This alignment with national resources acts like an antidote to the whims of the global energy market, providing a form of energy 'insulation.'

Take Denmark, for example, a nation that has harnessed its gusty winds to produce over 40% of its electricity demand. There's a nuanced elegance in how they've done it—through strategic investments and policy frameworks that prioritize sustainability and local energy production, Denmark has become a beacon of energy security. No longer hostage to oil prices or foreign gas supplies, Denmark enjoys a fortified energy independence that secures not only a stable grid but also a stable future.

From a broader perspective, energy independence through wind is also about risk mitigation. Diversifying energy sources helps buffer against supply disruptions, price spikes, and political entanglements associated with fossil fuel trade. In regions abundant in wind but lacking in conventional resources, wind energy can transform an economic liability into an asset, fostering self-reliance.

The national security implications are equally compelling. By diminishing reliance on foreign energy sources, countries reduce their exposure to transnational risks and the uncertainties of global supply chains. Energy independence becomes a strategic and pragmatic approach to national defense, liberating countries from energy-import vulnerabilities that could be exploited during international conflict or embargoes.

For countries with substantial wind potential, the path to security is not merely feasible but economically prudent. The levelized cost of electricity from wind has plummeted over the past decade, making it competitive even without subsidies. As wind projects continue to dot landscapes with little environmental compromise, they represent not just progress, but sovereignty—an assertion of energy control powered by nature.

Moreover, the implications of wind energy extend beyond individual nations, influencing regional stability and cooperation. As countries develop their wind potential, they foster interconnected power grids, champion cross-border energy projects, and engage in collaborative energy markets, enhancing regional security and stability in ways that fossil fuel independence fails to guarantee.

Nevertheless, transitioning to a wind-powered framework entails challenges that must be navigated thoughtfully. The variability of wind necessitates advances in grid management, energy storage solutions, and complementary energy sources like solar and hydroelectric power. These technological solutions are crucial to ensuring a consistent and secure energy supply.

As countries endeavor to fortify their energy independence and security, wind energy offers a visionary path forward. It entices with the prospect of a world less reliant on the caprices of fossil fuels—a world bolstered by domestic prowess and marked by resilience and stability. Wind energy is not merely an alternative; it is an enabler of sovereignty, ensuring that the power to shape our energy future is ours alone, flowing freely and indiscriminately from nature itself.

6.4 Renewable and Sustainable Source

In an age where sustainability dialogues fuel decisions about our planet's future, wind energy soars as a beacon of hope, emblematic of a shift towards renewable resources. With its capacity to reduce dependence on finite fuels and foster an eco-friendly energy paradigm, wind energy encapsulates the ethos of environmental stewardship and long-term use.

The concept of sustainability in energy resources is simple yet profound: meeting the needs of the present without compromising the ability of future generations to meet their own. Wind energy embodies this principle with an elegance that belies its mechanical complexity. At a fundamental level, it captures and converts a natural, inexhaustible resource into electricity—a dance with nature that reflects an entirely different energy narrative than that written by fossil fuels.

Unlike coal or oil, which are drawn from limited reserves meticulously formed over eons, wind is a product of solar radiation warming the atmosphere—meaning its "fuel" is as endless as the sun's lifecycle itself. This intrinsic renewability ensures that wind energy can be harnessed indefinitely, maintaining a steady course toward sustainability without fear of depletion.

Historically, humanity's romance with harnessing wind is not new. Sailors traversed the seas with wind-laden sails millennia ago, and the classic windmill—an icon of rustic efficiency—ground grains and pumped water with serene reliability. Modern wind turbines echo this heritage yet do so with technological sophistication that allows for significant contributions to our energy matrix.

As civilization has thrust forward, the issue of fossil fuel depletion has become a stark reality. It's a sobering thought that many of the reservoirs that once seemed boundless are approaching their twilight. In contrast, wind energy presents a future-facing solution where supply constriction is not in the lexicon, delivering sustained energy outputs without siphoning finite resources.

One of the keystones of wind energy's sustainability is land use. While turbines require space, they do not sport the heavy environmental footprints of traditional energy sources. Wind farms can comfortably coexist with agricultural activities below, enabling farmland to play a dual role in food and energy production. Such compatibility showcases wind energy's potential to augment, rather than supplant, other critical land uses.

The environmental benefits of wind turbines are amplified by their minimal pollution profile. Once operational, they emit no air or water pollutants— traits that further bolster their sustainable character. This absence of emissions not only contributes to cleaner air and water but also aligns wind energy with broader ecological conservation goals, supporting both biodiversity and human health.

Moving beyond environmental sustainability, the longevity of wind energy is affirmed by ongoing advancements in technology. The evolution of turbine design has seen significant improvements in efficiency, height, and capacity, allowing turbines to produce more energy and function in a broader array of wind conditions than ever before. This technological progress promises consistent and increasing returns on wind investments, ensuring their place in a long-term energy strategy.

Critically, the issue of sustainability also pivots on economic viability. The decreasing cost of wind energy generation is a testament to its economic sustainability. As technologies advance and production scales increase, the cost of wind power continues to decline, making it an attractive option for both investors and policymakers seeking both sustainability and economic prudence.

Furthermore, the holistic nature of wind energy production presents exciting avenues for research and development. Integrating cutting-edge materials, artificial intelligence for predictive maintenance, and enhanced grid interconnections represents a proactive approach to ensuring the resilience and adaptability of wind power systems.

Practical applications of these elements are visible worldwide. The integration of wind power into Denmark's energy grid, as explored earlier, serves as a living laboratory for the sustainable scale-up of wind resources. Elsewhere, large-scale projects like offshore wind farms illustrate how using untapped maritime spaces can further bolster energy supplies without impinging on terrestrial ecosystems.

In the face of climate change, exacerbated by unabated carbon emissions, wind energy contributes to sustainable mitigation strategies. By cutting emissions and reducing dependence on fossil fuels, wind power aligns with climate goals while preserving the integrity of ecosystems.   Its promise is one of maintaining ecological equilibrium—providing energy without relinquishing environmental health.

As an axis for sustainable energy policy, wind energy's potential for long-term use is unparalleled. It invites us to reimagine energy systems that will not only support contemporary needs but also empower future generations, allowing humanity to thrive harmoniously with the planet.

Wind energy, then, is not merely a component of the renewable energy conversation; it is a cornerstone of sustainable development. It brings forth a vision of energy autonomy that transcends present-day challenges, offering a renewable promise to underpin and empower a resilient, ecologically balanced, and prosperous future.

6.5   Community and Social Benefits

Wind energy is often celebrated for its environmental and economic contributions on a macro scale, but it's at the community level where its true impact can illuminate the path to a more integrated and progressive future. Wind projects harbor the capacity to transform local landscapes, not just through visual changes on the horizon but through deeper, more profound socio-economic developments that inject vibrancy into regions across the globe.

Picture a small rural town nestled amidst sprawling hills, its economy traditionally reliant on agriculture or extractive industries, now facing the relentless march of modern challenges—declining populations, scarce employment opportunities, and stagnant economic growth. Herein lies the potential for wind energy to become a catalyst for renewed hope and opportunity, seamlessly weaving economic and infrastructural development into the community's fabric.

The genesis of such transformation is rooted in the economic synergy generated by wind projects. These developments often require skilled labor for construction, operation, and maintenance—a boon for local job markets. From logistical planning to the physical installation of turbines, locals encounter a spectrum of employment opportunities across various skill levels, effectively turning wind energy into a lifeline for rural economies with otherwise limited avenues for growth.

Beyond direct employment, wind projects often instigate the revitalization of local businesses. Construction and maintenance workers spend money at local establishments such as stores, restaurants, and services, thus increasing local income and financial activity. Ancillary businesses, such as equipment suppliers, transport services, and hospitality sectors, also stand to gain from the influx of heightened commercial activity linked to wind energy development.

Layers of community benefit are further unspooled in the form of lease payments to landowners. For many farmers and ranchers, entering agreements with wind developers not only provides a regular and stable source of income but also helps mitigate market risks associated with agriculture, such as weather variability and fluctuating crop prices. Wind leases, therefore, function not only as economic lifelines but also as mechanisms of financial resilience for landowners.

However, the potential benefits of wind energy stretch beyond individual gain. Communities often witness improvements in infrastructure as developers invest in roads, grid connections, and other necessary facilities. These infrastructural upgrades can dovetail with broader public works, offering long-term utility far after initial construction phases are complete, further enhancing the quality of life for residents.

Moreover, wind energy projects frequently position themselves as community stakeholders, reinvesting in local areas through voluntary programs or partnerships. Developers contribute to community funds, educational scholarships, or local events, fostering a sense of reciprocity and shared growth.   By sponsoring local initiatives or facilities, such as schools or sports complexes, wind developers can enrich community life and sow seeds of long-lasting social value.

A profound illustration of these benefits can be found in the story of Spirit Lake, Iowa. Once facing economic stagnation, the introduction of wind energy into the local economy equated to the infusion of prosperity. Residents saw roads and schools improved, and community centers flourish, all while maintaining their close-knit societal bonds. This exemplifies how wind energy projects, when harmoniously integrated with local interests, can uplift communities in multifaceted ways.

Wind energy also invites cultural shifts, fostering community pride and environmental stewardship as residents become stakeholders in sustainable energy production.   This transition embodies more than physical infrastructure—it signals an ideological shift towards a sustainable identity, encouraging community-led discussions on environmental responsibility and renewable futures.

The wind industry's presence can synergize with tourism, promoting sites as eco-destinations for curious visitors who wish to witness renewable energy in action. This burgeoning sector provides yet another outlet for community growth, creating an ecosystem where education on sustainable practices fosters economic benefit.

Yet, the road to these benefits is not without challenges. Wind projects must be approached with genuine collaboration between developers and community stakeholders, ensuring that benefits are equitably distributed and local concerns heard. Transparent dialogues can ease apprehensions, such as environmental impacts, and ensure that renewable initiatives align with community values and visions.

Participation in such discussions breeds empowerment and ownership among locals, transforming wind energy projects from outside interventions to sources of communal pride. This cooperative spirit, when nurtured, forms the bedrock of successful project implementation that reverberates beyond mere economic metrics.

Thus, as we stand at the intersection of technological ingenuity and social cohesion, wind energy offers more than just a sustainable energy solution. It presents a model for community enrichment and development, lighting the way for an integrated approach where the power generated under wide, open skies fuels tangible human progress.

Wind energy represents a golden opportunity for communities seeking economic revitalization and infrastructure enhancement. As metaphoric bridges connecting modernity with tradition, wind projects encapsulate the potential to invigorate societal structures and enrich the human condition, demonstrating that sustainable energy solutions are indeed tailored for the communities that they power. Through wind energy, local horizons are not merely defined by turbine silhouettes but by a horizon of opportunity and shared prosperity.

Chapter 7

Challenges and Solutions in Wind Power

Wind power faces challenges such as intermittency, environmental impacts, and land use conflicts. Technological advancements, like improved storage solutions, help mitigate variability, while innovative designs reduce ecological disruption. Effective siting strategies address land concerns, and supportive policies and economic incentives enhance development. Overcoming these obstacles is essential for maximizing wind energy's contribution to the global energy landscape.

7.1   Intermittency and Reliability

The charm of wind lies in its capricious nature—dancing across landscapes, stirring seas and skies. However, this very capriciousness, reminiscent of a moody artist, presents a formidable challenge to those who rely on it for consistent energy production. This phenomenon, known as intermittency, highlights the inherent variability of wind, both in speed and direction, which affects the reliability of wind as an energy source.

Historically, societies have harnessed wind's power, yet these endeavors often echoed the unpredictability of the resource itself. Ancient mariners depended on favorable winds to navigate the seas, while early windmills tirelessly crushed grain or pumped water, yet faltered during still days. Today, the integration of wind into modern energy systems necessitates a nuanced understanding of its intermittency and how to mitigate its disruptive impacts.

The unpredictability of wind poses challenges primarily because an electrical grid requires a constant and balanced supply of electricity. Unlike traditional power stations—where operators can control output to match demand—wind turbines can only produce electricity when the wind is blowing. Not too fast; not too sluggish; it must be just right. It's this "Goldilocks effect" that complicates matters, as it demands a balancing act as intricate as keeping a kite steady during a turbulent breeze.

To better comprehend the intermittency challenge, imagine a bustling city fervently demanding electricity. Power plants tap into various energy sources to ensure lights remain on, hospitals operate, and so forth. Now, consider introducing our whimsical and somewhat unpredictable wind hero into this equation. A sudden lull or gust can upset the carefully maintained equilibrium needed to match electricity supply with demand in real time.

The reliability of wind energy is further compounded by the regional characteristics of wind patterns. Coastal areas might boast relatively steady maritime winds, while inland regions experience sporadic gusts. An exquisite dance of statistics and meteorological forecasting attempts to predict wind activity, but even with advanced models, certainty eludes our grasp.

Addressing such hurdles involves weaving a tapestry

from various threads of technological, structural, and inventive solutions. One of the most promising approaches lies in energy storage systems, designed to capture wind energy when it's plentiful and release it when the breeze subsides. Consider energy storage akin to a squirrel hoarding acorns. During a windy surplus, like the metaphorical squirrel, storage systems gather and store energy for leaner times.

Batteries, particularly lithium-ion variants, have become central pieces in the storage puzzle. While traditionally associated with consumer electronics, they now scale up to grid levels, deftly managing fluctuations inherent in renewable sources like wind. However, large-scale deployment necessitates overcoming cost, environmental impact, and resource availability challenges. Moreover, batteries offer short-term solutions—a matter of hours rather than weeks.

Enter the domain of pumped hydro storage, a concept dating back to 19th-century engineering ingenuity. This technique involves pumping water uphill into reservoirs when excess electricity is available, then releasing it downhill through turbines when energy demand peaks. While effective, the method's reliance on favorable topography and environmental considerations limits widespread application.

Similarly, green hydrogen has been heralded for its potential to bridge periods of intermittency. Here, surplus wind energy powers electrolysis, splitting water into oxygen and hydrogen, with the latter stored for subsequent use or converted back into electricity. The versatility of hydrogen—as both an energy carrier and constraint-free location storage—makes it an alluring technology. Scientists and engineers work diligently on cost reduction and efficiency optimization to elevate green hydrogen to broader practical viability.

107

Beyond storage, enhancements in grid infrastructure provide another route to manage wind variability. With sophisticated transmission networks, regions can share wind power, essentially borrowing it from wind-abundant locales during local shortages. It's akin to neighborly borrowing of a cup of sugar but on an electrical scale. However, upgrading transmission networks poses its own challenges, from high costs and logistical hurdles to political and regulatory intricacies.

Furthermore, diversification remains a steadfast strategy to combat intermittency. By synergizing wind with other renewable sources—such as solar, hydro, or geothermal—energy systems enhance their resilience. When the wind subsides, the sun may shine or vice versa, ensuring that at least some manner of natural energy graces the grid.

Ultimately, the imperative to harness and manage wind's whimsical power converges on innovation. Scientists and engineers labor ceaselessly, crafting solutions that bolster reliability without quelling the vital spirit that makes wind power supremely sustainable. In embracing wind's capriciousness and coupling it with technology and infrastructure, humans can stride confidently towards a future both powered by nature and respectful of its nuances.

In essence, mastering the art of wind energy involves not just serving today's gripping demand for sustainable power but creating harmony between humanity's energy aspirations and the planet's ecological rhythms. Amidst its challenges, wind whisperingly reminds us that its gifts are plentiful, provided we attune to its ever-shifting temperament.

7.2 Environmental and Wildlife Concerns

As the tall, slender figures of wind turbines stretch across landscapes and twirl in harmony with the sky, they symbolize our commitment to a cleaner, renewable future. Yet, one cannot overlook the paradox that often accompanies such symbols of progress: while these turbines contribute to reducing greenhouse gas emissions, their presence on natural landscapes raises pertinent environmental and wildlife concerns.

The advent of wind energy is not a modern phenomenon. Ancient civilizations harnessed wind for tasks ranging from grinding grain to sailing across oceans. Yet, as we pivot towards wind power in our quest for sustainable energy, we find ourselves called to balance technological advancement with ecological stewardship.

The potential environmental impact of wind farms begins with their construction. To install these massive structures, substantial land areas are often cleared, altering local habitats. This can lead to habitat fragmentation, where once-connected ecosystems become divided, hindering species' migration and breeding patterns. The act of clearing land for road construction, turbine bases, and power lines can disrupt soil and water dynamics, affecting local flora and fauna.

Moreover, once operational, wind turbines pose additional direct threats to certain wildlife—most notably birds and bats. Soaring gracefully through the skies, many bird species, particularly raptors, find themselves at risk of collision with turbine blades. Research indicates that the swift rotation of turbine blades can often be unseen by birds in flight until it is too late. Similarly, bats, whose echolocation capabilities

109

might not detect these rapidly moving objects, fall victim to this innovatively engineered peril.

But it's not all doom and gloom. Innovative minds continuously strive to mitigate these impacts, ensuring that our path to clean energy is as gentle as possible on the natural world. Various strategies are being explored and implemented to reduce the adverse effects of wind farms on local ecosystems.

Firstly, strategic siting of wind farms plays a crucial role. By selecting locations with minimal ecological sensitivity, developers can circumvent habitats home to vulnerable species. Furthermore, conducting thorough environmental impact assessments (EIAs) before construction aids in identifying potential ecological threats. These assessments not only spotlight possible environmental disturbances but also offer mitigation strategies to address them, allowing for informed decision-making.

In addition, technological innovations are at the forefront of these mitigation efforts. Radar and acoustic monitoring systems have been developed to detect the presence of birds and bats around wind farms. When such systems identify these creatures nearby, turbines can be temporarily halted or slowed down to reduce collision risks—a tactic sometimes referred to as "feathering" the turbines. These systems exemplify how technology can adapt to coexist peacefully with nature, much like tuning a finely crafted string instrument to the surrounding orchestra.

Moreover, considering turbine design and operation can lead to further integration of wind energy with the ecosystem. For instance, painting one of the turbine blades black has shown promising results in reducing avian fatalities, as it improves blade visibility against the sky. Adjustments to turbine operational patterns during peak migration periods or inclement weather can also lessen wildlife conflicts significantly.

Beyond birds and bats, wind farm operations can sometimes influence nearby oceanic life. Offshore wind farms, though less frequently associated with terrestrial wildlife concerns, present unique challenges to marine ecosystems. The underwater noise from construction and turbine operation can disturb aquatic life, particularly marine mammals that rely on sonar for communication and navigation. To mitigate these effects, developers may employ noise-reducing technologies like bubble curtains and time construction activities to avoid sensitive periods for marine species.

Moreover, the broader ecological impact of wind farms extends to their potential effects on landscapes and seascapes. Aesthetic considerations are not simply a human concern. Changes in landscape can influence local climate conditions and subsequently alter the habitats of indigenous species. For this reason, integrating ecological landscaping into wind farm development can help maintain local biodiversity and ecological roles.

As the debate over wind energy's environmental impact continues, the guiding principle should be one of balance. While the transition to renewable energy sources, such as wind power, is essential to combatting climate change, it must not come at the expense of biodiversity. With a thoughtful approach—integrating cutting-edge technology, careful planning, and environmental vigilance—we can minimize these impacts and foster a future where renewable energy and wildlife sustainability walk hand in hand.

Treading this path requires collaboration and open dialogue between developers, conservationists, policymakers, and local communities. By nurturing this dialogue, we emphasize not just the global imperative of cutting carbon emissions, but the shared responsibility to protect the diverse tapestry of life on Earth.

In this delicate dance of progress and preservation, the silhouettes of spinning turbines against the horizon serve as a testament to our aspirations—a reminder that we can, indeed, rise to the challenge of harmonizing with the natural world, and in doing so, achieve an energy revolution that resonates with both human innovation and the rhythms of nature.

7.3   Siting and Land Use Issues

Wind turbines, with their sleek, towering presence, strive to capture the ever-so-unpredictable breath of Zephyrus to churn out clean energy.   But as they reach for the skies, these structures inevitably land a significant footprint on the Earth, setting the stage for a complex ballet of land use and community dynamics.

At the heart of siting and land use issues lies the fundamental need for space.   Wind farms, unlike their fossil-fueled counterparts, are not confined to a discreet plot of land.   Instead, they expand across vast areas, with sufficient distance between turbines to ensure optimal efficiency. Thus begins the challenge of finding suitable tracts of land—those blessed with consistent and steady winds without trespassing into areas bordering environmental sensitivity or human habitation.

Historically, sprawling flatlands and breezy ridges have been prime real estate for wind farm installations owing to their unobstructed wind flow. Yet, when examining the true complexity behind land acquisition for wind projects, one must peel back the layers of geographical,

112

cultural, and regulatory elements.

First, consider the historical context. Land use has evolved, shaped by generations of agricultural practices, urban expansion, and conservation efforts. These human activities paint the backdrop against which wind projects now vie for space. As developers search for suitable landscapes, they are bound to navigate a mosaic of existing uses—farmland that feeds communities, pastures that support local economies, and conservation areas where flora and fauna flourish.

While on the surface, vast expanses of rural land seem ideal, land availability does not imply absence of contention. Agricultural communities often find themselves on the negotiation table, debating whether to share their territory with swaying turbines. The promise of lease payments and economic incentives shines brightly, yet is counterbalanced by concerns over land degradation and visual disruption.

Beyond the fields, the issue of public opposition emerges as a formidable layer of the siting debate. The human element—opinions, perceptions, and values—introduces a human-centered trial for siting efforts. Communities often express unease over the aesthetic impact of towering turbines altering cherished landscapes, an effect sometimes coyly dubbed the "not in my backyard" or NIMBY phenomenon.

Wind developers thus embark on a delicate tango with host communities. For projects to succeed, they must transcend mere transactional arrangements, fostering a genuine partnership with local residents. Effective communication, transparency, and community engagement transform adversarial stand-offs into collaborative dialogue. Decision-makers who prioritize understanding local cultural values and addressing concerns stand a greater chance at eliciting community buy-in.

Case studies abound, offering lessons in harmonious siting. Consider the collaborative approach adopted in Denmark, a vanguard of wind energy. Danish wind projects have long embraced cooperative ownership models, where rural stakeholders become part-owners of wind farms. This not only disperses the economic benefits but also fosters community pride and acceptance. Indeed, when individuals see themselves reflected in the spinning blades towering above, the sense of place and contribution transcends mere electrons flowing into the grid.

Regulatory frameworks further compound the siting puzzle. Different jurisdictions apply varied rules, ranging from national mandates to localized zoning regulations. Environmental impact assessments (EIAs), often legally required, scrutinize potential siting sites to mitigate ecological harm. These assessments, while essential, can embroil projects in lengthy permitting processes, where hurdles can emerge as readily as dandelions on a spring lawn.

Offshore wind projects, while alleviating some terrestrial concerns, are not immune to siting complexities. The vast seas offer boundless breezes, but maritime projects must navigate concerns from fishing industries, shipping routes, and ecological sensitivities inherent in marine environments. The struggle continues beneath the seabed, as developers confront issues linked to underwater cabling and subsea terrain.

In response to such challenges, spatial planning emerges as a critical strategy. By mapping existing land uses alongside wind resource data, decision-makers can identify zones for potential development that minimize conflicts and maximize wind production. These efforts are likened to fitting together a jigsaw puzzle, where each piece signifies diverse interests—ecological, economic, social—and how they intertwine within a landscape.

As we gaze towards the horizon of a wind-powered future, finding a truce between land availability and public sentiment remains paramount. Successful siting and land use strategies rest upon sensitivity to cultural landscapes, adaptive regulatory approaches, and the nurturing of community trust. At stake is not just the promise of clean energy, but a vision of sustainable coexistence, where progress marries place and people flourish alongside technology.

In this grand narrative of siting wind projects, we find ourselves revisiting fundamental human narratives—the stories of land ownership, stewardship, and community identity. Just as the ancients envisioned Aeolus harnessing the winds, modern societies innovate means to channel those timeless energies into a sustainable tomorrow, all the while honoring the landscapes that cradle these ambitious dreams.

7.4 Technological and Infrastructure Barriers

As wind turbines twirl vigorously in the dance of renewable energy, the rhythm is occasionally stuttered by the very structures and systems designed to support them. Technological and infrastructure barriers, unavoidable companions in this journey, often serve as the wind energy industry's reality check, calling for innovative leaps to sustain this grand performance of harnessing the breeze.

To understand these barriers, we must embark on a journey back in time to the chapters of technological evolution. Early wind energy attempts were rather humble, marked by clunky windmills slowly turning grain into flour. From those pioneers, today's towering behemoths have morphed into technological marvels; yet, the hurdles of enhancing efficiency, cost-effectiveness, and integration linger like tricky crosswinds.

At the heart of technology's quest is the goal of maximizing energy capture while minimizing costs. Wind turbines, ingenious though they are, face limitations in their evolution. One substantial barrier is the design itself—the quest for larger and more efficient turbines capable of harnessing more energy from the wind's fickle nature. Larger turbines can indeed capture more energy, yet they demand materials that withstand greater mechanical stress, ensuring these giants remain steadfast against the elements.

Here lie the intricacies of material science.   Future advancements hinge on the availability of lightweight, durable materials that make scaling up to larger blades feasible without incurring prohibitive costs. This pursuit involves innovating beyond traditional materials like fiberglass and steel, and instead delving into advanced composites—a task akin to alchemy where the philosopher's stone is cost-efficient durability.

For wind energy to realize its full potential, these turbines also need infrastructure that can handle both the spatial burden and the energy they produce. The grid represents a formidable competitor in this race. Current power grids were designed for centralized, fossil-fueled power generation, not for the dispersed, variable energy sources like wind. Integrating wind power thus requires both technological upgrades and strategic redesigns, transforming antiquated systems into a sophisticated tapestry of interconnected energy flows.

Consider the intricacies of the electrical grid, a mind-boggling web likened to a city's veins—a network distributing life-sustaining energy. Wind's inherent variability poses a challenge here, as existing grids were never quite outfitted for unpredictability. A surge of energy from a powerful gale or a lull on a peaceful afternoon necessitates instantaneously adjustable systems, lest the calm spell or stormy gust triggers a grid-wide imbalance.

Further complicating matters is the challenge of geography. Prime wind sites are often situated far from urban centers that demand energy in earnest. Connecting these remote outposts to the grid involves miles of transmission lines—an endeavor fraught with regulatory, environmental, and technical hurdles. The pursuit of improved power electronics and high-voltage direct current (HVDC) systems holds promise for efficiently bridging these expansive distances, but requires investment and innovation to leap from theory to practice.

Beyond the grid and distribution challenges looms the colossal barrier of storage. The capriciousness of wind demands that energy storage technology develop in tandem, ensuring steadiness in supply. Currently, available solutions such as lithium-ion batteries or pumped hydro storage remain expensive and limited in scope, underscoring the necessity for technological breakthroughs in capturing and storing wind in a cost-effective manner.

Perhaps an understated challenge lies in the need for skilled labor. A shortage of trained technicians and engineers who can build, maintain, and optimize sophisticated turbine and grid technology poses a threat. Investing in education and training programs becomes imperative to ensure that future generations possess the expertise to engineer, design, and sustain the demanding infrastructure of wind energy.

In addressing these barriers, international collaborations and public-private partnerships shine as beacons on the path forward. Countries piloting advanced technology projects—be it in turbine design, grid modernization, or storage capacity—create models that others can emulate. Knowledge transfer across borders serves to accelerate progress, a testament to the premise that renewable energy bears no allegiance to national boundaries.

The question, then, remains: how do we vault over these technological and infrastructure hurdles? The answer is what some refer to as "incremental innovations"—a series of small yet impactful advancements rather than elusive breakthroughs. It is a reminder that even the most daunting barriers can be surmounted with steady, determined progress, much like ascending a mountain with patient and purposeful steps.

In this symphony of wind energy, technology and infrastructure operate as both challenge and opportunity. Developing systems that effectively harness and distribute wind energy, while balancing costs and efficiency, may indeed seem like conducting an orchestra without an overtone of cacophony. Yet, therein lies the marvel—a testament to human ingenuity and resilience in the face of a challenge as dynamic and changeable as the very wind we endeavor to capture.

As this tale of technological evolution unfolds, it underscores humanity's capacity to dream beyond the visible horizon. In overcoming these barriers, we secure not just an energy source, but a future propelled by the persistent pursuit of innovation, guided by the timeless rhythm of windswept progress.

7.5   Economic and Policy Challenges

In the dynamic dance of wind energy development, economic and policy challenges appear as tango partners wrestling for dominance, often dictating the pace of advancement. Wind energy, while offering the promise of a clean and eternal source of power, must navigate the choppy financial waters and kaleidoscopic policy landscapes before it can successfully take root.

Imagine, if you will, the world of finance—the intricate web of market forces, investment flows, and economic forecasts. Here, wind energy must prove itself not just as an environmental boon, but as a viable economic contender. Initial investment costs for wind energy infrastructure can be daunting, especially compared to traditional fossil fuel setups with established networks and technologies. High upfront costs for wind turbines, site preparation, and grid integration cast long shadows of hesitation among investors.

Consider the vast array of stakeholders peering into the crystal ball of wind energy: private investors looking for returns, governments aligned with policy imperatives, and companies juggling costs against corporate social responsibility. Each of these players approaches the table with distinct interests and concerns, all seeking some assurance of wind energy's financial promise.

Incentivizing investment requires a delicate balance of financial tools and mechanisms. Enter stage left, government subsidies and tax credits—a financial lifeline for the burgeoning wind sector. These fiscal instruments counterbalance the steep initial costs, making wind power more appealing to investors and boosting its competitive edge against heavily-subsidized fossil fuels. Countries like Germany and the United States have leveraged production tax credits (PTCs) and

119

feed-in tariffs to stimulate their wind industries, betting on long-term economic and environmental dividends.

However, reliance on subsidies brings its own tensions. Political winds can shift abruptly, altering or removing supports that the industry may have heavily factored into their economic calculus. Moreover, debates arise about when and how to transition from government dependency to market competitiveness—a complex pas de deux requiring timing, grace, and precision.

Regulatory policies also weave a compelling narrative in this dynamic story. The process of permitting and compliance lays down a waltz of patience and perseverance for project developers. Lengthy permitting processes, mired in bureaucratic inefficiencies, can delay projects and escalate costs. Each layer of regulatory approval adds complexity, demanding keen understanding of national, regional, and even local policies that affect every spinning blade and planted pole.

A promising solution to these regulatory labyrinths lies in streamlining and harmonizing policy frameworks—a one-stop-shop approach for permits that can reduce red tape and accelerate project timelines. This requires collaboration across governmental levels and agencies— akin to aligning the diverse sections of an orchestra to ensure a harmonious rendition.

Furthermore, international cooperation can create fertile grounds for wind energy by establishing globally recognized standards, thus easing cross-border investments and fostering technology transfer. This cooperation positions wind energy within the broader scheme of global climate commitments, aligning national policies with international sustainability goals.

Economic models that embrace risk-sharing also stand

out in facilitating wind development. Power purchase agreements (PPAs), allowing wind energy producers to sell electricity at fixed prices, offer stable income streams to investors. Through this financial innovation, electricity prices are locked, insulating projects from the vicissitudes of market fluctuations—a soothing balm for investors' anxieties.

Yet, let us not forget the human element twirling alongside these economic and policy challenges. Public perception and acceptance of wind projects tie back to local socio-economic contexts. Community benefits agreements (CBAs) and cooperative ownership models narrate empowering tales of residents partaking in and profiting from wind development, ensuring economic integration and broad-based support.

Among the economic and policy waltz emerges an unlikely chorus: the story of job creation and economic revitalization. The wind industry boasts a broad array of roles—from engineers, technicians, and construction workers to legal advisors and environmental consultants. Each role contributes to an eco-centric economic shift, enticing stakeholders with prospects of diversification and resilience.

As wind energy flirts with the scales of economy and equity, the global stage presents diverse scenarios. Developing nations view wind energy as a vehicle for economic development, rooting energy security and poverty alleviation within an equitable framework. Here, inclusive financing mechanisms and international aid can nurture local wind industries, ensuring they contribute to a sustainable and prosperous future.

In this dance of dollars and policy, wind energy finds itself on the exhilarating edge of economic transformation. Addressing barriers in this domain demands creative choreography—a duet of innovation and policy foresight that transcends traditional limitations.   As new chapters of wind energy unfold, its allure becomes ever more intertwined with our collective ambitions for a greener, more stable global economy.

In the vast arena of energy production, wind's pivotal role is underscored by these economic and policy aspirations. The future, though it beckons, whispers caution—imploring stakeholders to step wisely but surely through the corridors of change, ensuring that wind energy's financial and regulatory ambitions twist elegantly into reality.

Chapter 8

The Future of Wind Energy

The future of wind energy is buoyed by technological advances enhancing efficiency and integration with other renewables. Anticipated market growth is driven by decreasing costs and increasing demand for clean energy. Strategic policies will support its expansion, positioning wind as a crucial component of a decarbonized global energy system. These developments promise to augment its role in achieving sustainable energy goals worldwide.

8.1   Technological Advancements

Harnessing the power of the wind has its roots deep in human history, a legacy stretching back to the first sailboats edging across ancient seas. However, modern wind energy's trajectory is characterized by rapid technological evolution aimed at efficiently capturing more energy from every gust. As the demand for efficient and scalable clean energy solutions continues to rise globally, the innovations in wind technology are more vital than ever.

Turbine Designs and Materials

One of the most significant areas of advancement in wind technology is the continual refinement of turbine designs and the materials from which they are constructed. Wind turbines have come a long way since the early days, with today's designs focusing on maximizing efficiency and minimizing wear. The adoption of lightweight composite materials allows for larger blades that can sweep more area without adding prohibitive weight. These newer materials are not only more durable, reducing maintenance needs, but also enhance overall aerodynamic performance.

Moreover, innovations like the vertical-axis wind turbine (VAWT) pose exciting alternatives to the traditional horizontal design. VAWTs can capture wind from any direction without needing to adjust their orientation. This quality makes them particularly attractive in urban environments or offshore settings where wind patterns can change abruptly.

Smart Turbines and IoT Integration

The integration of Internet of Things (IoT) technology into wind farms is a game-changer. Smart turbines are now equipped with sensors that collect vast amounts of data on wind speed, direction, temperature, and turbine performance. This real-time data is analyzed to optimize the turbine's angle and rotation speed, ensuring they operate at maximum efficiency. Such technology not only enhances energy capture but also preemptively identifies maintenance needs, significantly reducing downtime and operational costs.

Predictive maintenance algorithms powered by artificial intelligence (AI) use this data to foresee potential mechanical issues before they manifest. This capability is particularly useful offshore, where maintenance is logistically complex and expensive.

Floating Wind Farms

Perhaps one of the most visionary advancements is the development of floating wind farms. Traditional offshore wind farms are limited to shallow waters due to the necessity of fixed seabed foundations. Floating wind farms, however, are buoyant platforms anchored to the seabed, enabling deployment in deeper waters with stronger and more consistent wind. This technology vastly expands the potential sites for offshore wind farms, alleviating competition for space in coastal zones and tapping into powerful wind resources far from shore.

The technological nuances involved in stabilizing these floating platforms against the often tumultuous sea environment remain a focus of research and development. Nevertheless, successful pilot projects have already demonstrated their viability and potential economic benefits.

Energy Storage and Grid Integration

The fluctuating nature of wind energy production has always posed significant challenges in terms of energy storage and grid integration. Innovations in battery technology and energy storage systems (ESS) provide critical solutions. Modern lithium-ion batteries, while dominant, are complemented by flow batteries and even more novel technologies like compressed air or pumped hydro storage, which are being refined for efficiency and scalability.

Moreover, advancements in smart grid technology empower better modulation of electricity flow, ensuring that surplus wind energy can be stored or redirected efficiently. Power electronics, such as advanced inverters, play a pivotal role in integrating wind power smoothly into the grid, maintaining stability and frequency even with its variable nature.

Advanced Control Systems

The future of wind turbine technology also hinges on sophisticated control systems that can adapt dynamically to changing conditions. Advanced control algorithms allow turbines to respond swiftly to shifts in wind speed and direction, maximizing efficiency and reducing mechanical stress. These adaptive controls are a crucial aspect of modern turbine technology, continuously learning and improving from operational data.

The implementation of inclusive control strategies extends beyond individual turbines to entire wind farms. Coordinated control systems enable a group of turbines to operate collectively, optimizing overall performance rather than that of each turbine in isolation. This approach is essential in sprawling wind farms where local wind conditions may vary considerably.

Environmental and Visual Considerations

While efficiency reigns supreme in wind technology, environmental and social acceptability remains crucial. Technologists are working towards minimizing the ecological footprint of wind farms. Innovations aim to minimize the impact on local wildlife, especially birds and bats. Ultrasonic dispersal devices and visually inconspicuous paint designs are part of the efforts to mitigate these impacts.

Furthermore, to address aesthetic concerns, particularly in picturesque rural and coastal areas, there is burgeoning interest in architectural turbine designs that blend harmoniously with their surroundings. Invisible turbines made with materials that become see-through in certain lighting conditions, for example, are being explored to reduce visual obtrusiveness.

The horizon for wind energy technology is brimming

with potential. From advanced materials and smart systems to floating farms and grid innovations, each technological leap pushes the envelope of what is possible, promising ever more efficient and sustainable energy production. These innovations not only enhance wind power's economic viability but also its capacity to meet the growing global demand for clean energy. As technology continues to advance, wind energy stands poised to play a pivotal role in driving the world toward a more sustainable and resilient energy future.

8.2 Global Market Trends

The winds of change are not just a metaphorical expression in the energy world but a literal one, as the global market for wind energy is swelling with unprecedented vigour. The last few decades have seen wind power transform from a niche player to a pivotal force in the global energy mix. This evolution is driven by a whirlwind of factors—economic, technological, and political—converging to shape the future of renewable energy. Understanding these market dynamics offers us a lens through which to anticipate the future trajectory of wind energy on a global scale.

The Rise of Emerging Markets

Traditionally dominated by a few key players such as the United States and European countries, the wind energy sector is now witnessing a robust proliferation into emerging markets. Nations in Latin America, Asia, and Africa are increasingly harnessing wind resources, incentivized by dropping technology costs and the urgent need to meet growing energy demands sustainably.

China stands as a towering figure in this narrative, having emerged as the largest installer of wind power capacity, propelled by aggressive governmental policies and substantial investment in renewable technologies. India follows closely, leveraging its vast landscapes and conducive wind corridors, particularly in regions like Tamil Nadu and Gujarat, which have become focal points for wind energy development.

Latin America's wind power potential is also being unlocked, with countries such as Brazil and Mexico capitalizing on strong wind currents to foster energy security and stimulate economic growth. Similarly, South Africa is spearheading wind projects to diversify its energy portfolio away from coal dependency.

Economic Influences

The economic rationale for expanding wind energy capacity is compelling, underpinning many of the observed trends. Wind power has seen a drastic reduction in costs due to technological innovations and increased economies of scale. This trend is expected to continue, as advances in turbine technology and materials, as discussed in earlier sections, further drive efficiency gains and cost reductions.

Moreover, the wind energy sector has become a significant employment driver, promising thousands of jobs in manufacturing, installation, and maintenance. This economic stimulus is particularly attractive to countries facing high unemployment rates, providing a multifaceted boost to local economies.

Policy and Political Dynamics

Policymakers worldwide are increasingly setting ambitious renewable energy targets as part of broader climate strategies, recognizing wind energy's pivotal role in reducing greenhouse gas emissions. Incentives such as feed-in tariffs, renewable portfolio standards, and carbon pricing mechanisms are catalyzing wind power investments.

Key international agreements, like the Paris Accord, serve as crucial policy frameworks that foster international cooperation and commitment towards expanding renewable energy. The proliferation of renewable energy auctions in various countries, where wind power often emerges as the lowest-cost option, further underscores the sector's growing competitiveness and appeal.

However, geopolitical factors and policy uncertainty remain inherent risks, with shifts in governmental priorities and international relations potentially influencing market dynamics. The challenge lies in ensuring continuity and stability in policy frameworks that maintain investor confidence and long-term development trajectories.

Offshore Wind Developments

A striking trend in the global market is the rise of offshore wind projects. While historically concentrated in Europe, with countries such as the UK, Germany, and Denmark leading the way, offshore wind is gaining traction in new territories. The allure of consistent, robust winds in offshore environments, combined with decreasing costs, is appealing to countries with extensive coastlines.

For instance, the United States is making significant strides to build its offshore capacity, especially along the East Coast. Similarly, Asia is not far behind, with Japan and Taiwan advancing substantial offshore wind development plans. These trends reflect a broader recognition of the potential for offshore wind to contribute significantly to national energy goals.

Challenges and Future Outlook

Despite the buoyant growth prospects, the wind energy sector faces several hurdles. Grid integration remains a challenge, requiring advanced infrastructure and smart grid technologies to manage variable energy inputs effectively. Moreover, land use conflicts and public opposition—often tied to aesthetic concerns—can impede wind farm siting and development.

Financing remains another significant concern, especially in emerging markets where financial systems may not be as robust. Mobilizing investment to meet the scale of the required infrastructure continues to be a formidable task.

However, the future outlook for wind energy is overwhelmingly positive. Continued research and innovation, coupled with strong policy support and market adaptation to changing conditions, are expected to catalyze further growth. The rise of hydrogen fuel technology, powered by wind energy, offers an exciting horizon, potentially transforming energy storage and distribution frameworks.

The global market for wind energy is at a pivotal intersection of opportunity and innovation. With sustained commitment from governments, the private sector, and international organizations, wind power can become a cornerstone of sustainable energy, driving economic prosperity while addressing the urgent challenge of climate change. As these trends unfold, they promise a transformative era for wind energy, poised to reshape the global energy landscape fundamentally.

8.3 Integration with Other Renewable Sources

Innovation in renewable energy doesn't stop at improving individual technology like wind turbines or solar panels—it's about creating a symphony of renewable energy sources that harmonize to power the world sustainably. The journey toward a comprehensive energy mix necessitates rolling up the sleeves and figuring out how different renewables can work together, seamlessly blending solar, wind, biomass, hydroelectric, and geothermal energies into a balanced grid.

The Complementary Nature of Solar and Wind Energy

Wind and solar power are widely recognized as the twin pillars of modern renewable energy infrastructure. They complement each other beautifully: when the wind isn't blowing, the sun is often shining, and vice versa. This symbiosis reduces the variability of renewable output and provides a more consistent energy supply.

Consider California, for instance, where solar energy faces ample opportunities during the summer afternoons, while the state experiences strong winds come evening. This natural shift can be leveraged to balance the demand curve and provide a smoother energy flow to the grid. The integration of solar and wind energy helps in flattening the infamous duck curve—a graphical representation of energy demand that can cause grid instability.

Hybrid Renewable Energy Systems

To capitalize on the strengths of various power sources, hybrid renewable energy systems are garnering attention. These systems combine two or more types of renewable energy into a single installation, ensuring

131

a diverse and consistent power output. For example, hybrid solar-wind farms offer significant efficiency improvements over standalone systems, reducing reliance on energy storage and enhancing grid stability.

Places with varying geographical conditions, like islands, are ideal candidates for such systems. For example, a hybrid setup could couple wind turbines with solar panels and batteries, using smart control systems to optimize energy flow based on real-time conditions.

Storage: The Great Equalizer

While the pairing of renewables is essential, energy storage technologies serve as the linchpin that solidifies this integration. By storing excess energy generated during peak periods of production, batteries, pumped hydroelectric storage, and other systems can release energy when output is low or demand is high.

Implementations of robust energy storage are expanding, such as Tesla's Powerwall installations that link with rooftop solar panels. These batteries allow households to store solar energy during the day and tap into it at night or during low sunlight periods. On a larger scale, advances in energy storage will play an instrumental role in accommodating fluctuations from both wind and solar power, ensuring reliability and consistency across regions.

Grid Modernization and Smart Technologies

An increasing reliance on intermittent renewables like wind and solar necessitates grid modernization. By embedding smart technologies within the grid infrastructure, operators can efficiently integrate multiple energy sources. Smart grids utilize real-time data and advanced computer algorithms to adapt swiftly to changes in energy demand and supply, optimizing energy distribution.

Demand response programs, for example, adjust the energy consumption patterns based on availability, aligning production from wind and solar with consumer needs. Such innovations are especially critical as they transform passive grids into dynamic ecosystems capable of adjusting to complex and dynamic energy flows.

Integrating with Other Renewables: Tapping into Mother Nature's Toolbox

Beyond wind and solar, other renewable resources like hydroelectric, geothermal, and biomass provide additional layers of energy diversity. Hydroelectric plants, often referred to as the "battery" of renewable energies, offer consistent power and operational flexibility. They can ramp production up or down rapidly in response to grid demand, playing a crucial supporting role.

Geothermal energy, sourced from the Earth's internal heat, and biomass, derived from organic materials, further balance the renewable mix by providing constant baseload power. These renewable sources may not be as scalable or widespread as wind or solar, but they add invaluable stability and adaptability to the grid.

Various countries are already demonstrating the effectiveness of integrated renewable systems. Take Germany, a pioneer in the renewable push, which uses a combination of solar, wind, and biogas energy to provide a substantial portion of its national energy needs. Utilizing subsidies and innovative grid solutions, Germany works toward a predominantly renewable energy mix.

Denmark, another leader in the sector, benefits immensely from its windy terrain. By integrating wind energy with combined heat and power stations and employing heat pumps, the country aims to achieve near-complete renewable energy supply by 2050. Meanwhile, Costa Rica leverages its prolific geothermal and hydroelectric resources, coupled with wind energy, to generate nearly all of its electricity from renewables.

Integrating various renewable sources intelligently is paramount for navigating the challenges of climate change and energy transition. The relationships between solar, wind, and other renewable resources are dynamic and synergistic, each adding its strengths to the equation. As grid technologies improve and energy storage breakthroughs occur, we inch closer to a fully renewable-powered world.

The future isn't simply about swapping fossil fuels for wind or solar; it's about weaving a tapestry of diverse renewable sources, each filling its unique role in generating a resilient and sustainable energy landscape. As energy systems evolve, their ability to adapt and integrate different renewables will determine the ease and success with which we transition to a greener future.

8.4   Role in a Decarbonized Future

In the quest for a sustainable future, the decarbonization of the global energy system shines as a beacon of necessity. Among the varied solutions, wind energy stands prominent, a formidable ally in reducing carbon emissions while meeting humanity's ever-growing energy needs. To truly appreciate wind energy's role in achieving climate targets, we must first delve into its benefits and explore how it seamlessly slots into a low-carbon framework.

Wind Energy: A Zero-Emissions Powerhouse

At its core, wind energy epitomizes a zero-emissions powerhouse during operation. Once turbines are spinning in the breeze, they generate electricity sans the pollutants associated with burning fossil fuels. This fundamental characteristic makes wind power an invaluable contributor to reducing greenhouse gas emissions—a crucial factor when confronting climate change.

Consider the IPCC's warning that global temperatures must not rise beyond 1.5°C above pre-industrial levels to prevent catastrophic climate impacts. In this context, wind energy's potential to displace fossil fuel generation while meeting increasing electricity demands is ever more critical. As countries race to slash emissions according to their pledges under the Paris Agreement, the expansion of wind power becomes an essential strategy in their decarbonization toolkits.

Economic Benefits and Cost-Effectiveness

The economic incentives tied to wind energy amplify its attractiveness in a decarbonized future. As highlighted in previous sections, the cost of wind energy has plummeted, making it one of the most cost-effective sources of new electricity generation. This affordability eases the economic transition for countries facing the dual pressures of reducing emissions and maintaining economic growth.

Furthermore, wind power generates numerous employment opportunities across the supply chain, from manufacturing and distribution to installation and maintenance. These avenues of employment support economic resilience in transitioning from fossil fuels to renewable energy, particularly in regions traditionally reliant on coal and oil industries.

Decentralization and Energy Independence

Wind energy, with its ability to be harnessed both on-shore and offshore, offers countries a path toward energy independence by decentralizing power generation. This decentralization reduces reliance on imported fossil fuels, thereby enhancing energy security—a significant concern for many nations wary of geopolitical tensions affecting energy supplies.

The adaptability of wind turbines to various environments also allows for innovative applications, such as community-owned wind farms. These projects not only empower local economies but also promote the democratization of energy production, encouraging public engagement in sustainability initiatives.

Environmental Advantages and Biodiversity

While the primary focus of wind energy's contribution to a decarbonized future rests on its carbon reduction capability, its broader environmental impacts warrant attention. Notably, wind energy requires relatively small land footprints for the infrastructure involved, leaving surrounding areas available for agriculture or conservation efforts—a symbiotic approach to land use that can be crucial in densely populated or agricultural regions.

Environmental considerations extend to biodiversity, where careful placement and technological advancements can mitigate potential impacts on wildlife. Strategies such as radar technology to shut down turbines when large flocks of birds approach are examples of ongoing efforts to harmonize wind energy with ecological well-being.

Integration with Novel Technologies

Achieving a decarbonized future doesn't rely solely on existing technologies but also on innovative integrations. Wind energy is at the forefront of such integration, pairing well with emerging technologies like green hydrogen production. Using excess wind power to electrolyze water into hydrogen offers a means of storing energy and providing a clean fuel source for sectors hard to decarbonize—transportation, shipping, and industrial processes.

Moreover, wind energy's role is buttressed by smart grid developments, leveraging big data and machine learning to forecast wind patterns and improve energy management across the grid. This innovation not only enhances efficiency but also smooths out the intermittency challenges that renewables like wind and solar typically face.

Global and Local Examples: Pathways Forward

The global map is dotted with tangible examples of wind energy paving the way toward decarbonization. In Denmark, wind turbines harnessed approximately 47% of the country's electricity by 2019, showcasing a powerful model of national commitment to renewable energy. This achievement aligns with Denmark's ambitious climate goals, aiming for net-zero emissions by 2050, with wind energy continuing to be a cornerstone of its strategy.

Elsewhere, the United Kingdom's substantial offshore wind farms in the North Sea—some of the largest in the world—demonstrate leadership in reducing carbon footprints while capitalizing on geographical advantages. These projects not only meet domestic energy needs but also position the UK as a leader in exporting renewable technologies and expertise.

Looking to the Future

Wind energy is poised to rise even further in prominence, particularly as technological improvements continue to drive down costs and enhance efficiency. Extensive global cooperation, investment in infrastructure, and public and private sector partnerships are all necessary to leverage wind energy's full potential.

The transition to a low-carbon future will require a tapestry of solutions—wind energy woven alongside solar, hydro, and nascent technologies. As a dynamic and evolving energy source, wind will undoubtedly play a pivotal role in achieving the global climate goals that protect our planet's future.

In sum, the promise of wind power lies not just in turbines turning in the wind but in its profound capacity to power our lives while preserving the natural world. As we stand at the cusp of an energy revolution, wind energy is not just a participant—it is a leader in the march toward a decarbonized world.

8.5   Policy and Strategic Developments

In the grand chessboard of global energy, policymakers and strategists wield significant influence, guiding the deployment and success of renewable energy initiatives. For wind energy—a front-runner in clean technology—crafted legislation and strategic vision are essential to unleash its full potential. As the world pivots towards a low-carbon future, understanding the policy landscape that drives wind energy expansion becomes imperative.

Historical Context: The Roots of Wind Policy

Historically, policy initiatives in the late 20th and early 21st centuries experienced varying degrees of success in stimulating wind energy. Early adopters like Denmark and Germany demonstrated foresight, implementing feed-in tariffs (FiTs) to guarantee a return on renewable investments, ultimately propelling wind technology forward. These policies inspired global counterparts, translating ambition into action and creating fertile ground for wind energy's maturation.

In the United States, tax incentives such as the Production Tax Credit (PTC) have provided crucial support for wind projects. However, the periodic expiration and renewals of such incentives reflect an ebb and flow nature, underscoring the need for stable, long-term policy frameworks to foster continuous sector growth.

The Modern Policy Landscape

Recent trends underscore an escalating global commitment to wind energy. National targets embedded within overarching climate strategies increasingly recognize wind power as a linchpin technology. However, the true measure of policy success lies in aligning governmental ambitions with actionable and sustainable frameworks.

Implementing streamlined permitting processes is vital. Lengthy and cumbersome approval procedures can stymie development. By adopting clear, efficient regulations—particularly regarding environmental and community impact assessments—governments can reduce bottlenecks, accelerating project timelines.

In addition, grid expansion and modernization remain central to integrating widespread wind energy. Scaling up wind energy requires adapting grid infrastructures to handle increased capacity and fluctuating inputs. Investment in smart technologies and interconnection capabilities is pivotal—a focus that requires legislative backing to secure funding and strategic alignment.

Incentives and Economic Instruments

To invigorate investment, economic instruments like sub-sidies, tax breaks, and renewable credits play fundamental roles. The European Union's Renewable Energy Directive exemplifies a policy commitment that compels member states to legally binding renewable energy targets, fostering regional collaboration and market confidence.

Moreover, carbon pricing mechanisms—whether via carbon taxes or cap-and-trade systems—indirectly support wind energy by making carbon-intensive power generation alternatives financially less attractive. By internalizing the cost of emissions, these policies level the playing field, creating competitive advantages for renewable projects.

Strategic National and International Initiatives

Countries setting bold national renewable goals send a definitive signal of intent to industry stakeholders. For instance, China's 2060 carbon neutrality pledge underscores a strategic shift towards renewables, evidenced by their outstripping wind power capacity records. Similarly, India's commitment to achieving 175 GW of renewable capacity by 2022 exemplifies an assertive national strategy garnering global attention.

On the international front, collaborations and alliances further buttress strategic thrusts. Organizations such as the International Renewable Energy Agency (IRENA) and initiatives like Mission Innovation mobilize resources and knowledge-sharing, elevating wind energy as a shared global pursuit.

Community and Public Engagement

Securing local community buy-in and fostering public support are indispensable strategy components. Public goodwill is built on transparency, consultation, and the demonstration of wind projects' socioeconomic benefits. Strategies such as community ownership models and benefit-sharing arrangements engender pride, trust, and broader acceptance.

By incorporating public input into project design and implementation, wind energy initiatives embody participatory democracy, shifting the narrative from "imposed" infrastructure to "community-driven" success stories. Countries like Scotland have witnessed positive outcomes from empowering communities to actively participate in clean energy projects.

Anticipated Policy Shifts

Looking forward, policies are expected to focus on smoothing the transition towards increasingly ambitious renewable targets. This may involve introducing adaptable regulatory frameworks responsive to industry insights and innovations—facilitating the deployment of offshore and floating wind technologies as discussed earlier.

Moreover, the intersection of digital technologies with energy policy presents opportunities for refined demand-side management. Transitioning to dynamic grid tariffs, for example, would incentivize consumption patterns aligned with wind output variability, further integrating renewable energy into daily life.

The policy and strategic landscape for wind energy is a dynamic tapestry, constantly evolving to meet the challenges of the modern world. By fostering innovation, investment, and inclusivity, policymakers create a fertile ground for wind energy not merely to grow but to thrive. With a careful balance of visionary ambition and pragmatic implementation, wind energy policies can drive robust growth, ensuring these mighty turbines continue their journey, propelling us toward a cleaner, more sustainable future.

Chapter 9

Wind Energy and the Environment

Wind energy significantly reduces carbon emissions, contributing to climate change mitigation. While concerns about wildlife impacts, such as bird and bat collisions, exist, strategies to minimize these effects are being implemented. Noise levels and land use issues are comparatively low, making wind a sustainable choice. Effective environmental management ensures wind energy's development harmonizes with ecosystem preservation, reinforcing its role as an environmentally responsible energy source.

9.1   Carbon Footprint Reduction

In the grand tapestry of climate change mitigation, wind energy emerges as a striking presence, weaving a tale of innovation and sustainability. As our global society grapples with escalating environmental crises, the importance of reducing greenhouse gas emissions becomes paramount. Enter the silent but powerful hero: wind energy. It might seem that the swaying blades on wind turbines echo the whispers of a bygone era, where mills harnessed nature's breath to grind grain or pump water. Yet today, these modern marvels stand as bastions of clean energy, contributing significantly to slashing our carbon footprint.

The essence of wind energy's charm lies in its fundamental operation. Wind turbines capture kinetic wind energy, transforming it into mechanical energy, which is then converted into electricity. Unlike their fossil-fueled counterparts, wind turbines generate power without emitting carbon dioxide (CO_2) during operation. This crucial difference underscores their role in the fight against climate change.

Consider for a moment the lifecycle of a traditional coal-fired power plant. From extraction and transportation to combustion, every phase contributes to the release of CO_2 and other greenhouse gases (GHGs) into our atmosphere. By contrast, wind energy sidesteps these emissions at nearly every turn. While there are carbon costs associated with manufacturing, transporting, and installing wind turbines, these are dwarfed by the ongoing emissions from fossil fuels. Indeed, once operational, a wind turbine offsets the CO_2 used in its construction within mere months of clean energy generation.

To understand the full impact of wind energy on our carbon footprint, one can look to the achievements of countries and regions that have embraced wind power. Denmark provides an enlightening case study. This Scandinavian nation has invested heavily in wind infrastructure, allowing it to meet over 40% of its electricity needs with wind as of recent years. The result? A significant reduction in national CO_2 emissions and a testament to the potential of wind as a cornerstone of a sustainable energy strategy.

The story doesn't end there. Wind energy also plays a critical role in modernizing energy systems. As more grids incorporate wind power, they reduce their reliance on fossil fuels, leading to sustained declines in GHG emissions. This transition to renewables, bolstered by advancements in smart grid technology, also supports a reduction in electricity wastage and further curbs emissions.

This commitment to wind energy isn't merely driven by climate ambitions but also by economics. The cost of wind energy has plummeted over the past decade. In many parts of the world, wind now stands as one of the cheapest sources of electricity. This economic viability further accelerates the transition to clean energy, making it not only an environmental imperative but a rational economic choice. With falling costs, the expansion of wind energy becomes an even more attractive proposition for governments and industries alike.

Yet, to truly appreciate wind energy's contribution, we must also consider the broader societal role it can play. In regions endowed with strong, consistent winds, investment in wind farms can foster local economies by creating jobs in construction, maintenance, and manufacturing. This helps build communities and infrastructure resilient in the face of a changing climate.

Furthermore, wind energy's expansion also encourages innovation. For instance, research into minimizing the carbon and resource footprints of turbine production continues to advance. Efforts are underway to develop blades that are easier to recycle and materials that are more sustainable. Such innovations promise to further diminish the lifecycle emissions of wind turbines, amplifying their environmental benefits.

However, while wind energy is a critical tool in reducing carbon emissions, a holistic approach is necessary. It must be part of a diversified strategy that includes other renewables, energy efficiency measures, and novel technologies such as carbon capture and storage. Wind energy serves as an anchor in this portfolio, providing the stability needed to reduce reliance on carbon-intensive sources and thus lowering the overall GHG emissions of our energy systems.

So, next time you encounter the towering presence of a wind turbine, reflect on its quiet revolution. Here stands a symbol of progress, casting a long shadow over the technologies of old, and paving the way for a carbon-neutral future. As the winds of change swirl around us, wind energy propels us towards a cleaner, more sustainable world. Embracing its potential is not just an environmental necessity but a beacon of hope as we sail into uncertain waters, charting a course toward resilience and sustainability.

9.2   Impact on Wildlife and Habitats

Amidst the rolling hills and vast plains where wind turbines stand tall, one might ask: what do these mechanical giants mean for the creatures with whom they share their landscapes? As we harness the power of the wind, ensuring that our renewable path aligns with the needs of the natural world is paramount. The interplay between wind farms and wildlife, particularly birds and bats, challenges us to strike a harmonious balance between technological progress and ecological preservation.

In the early days of wind energy development, the impact on wildlife was often uncharted territory, an afterthought in the rush towards renewables. Stories of bird fatalities in regions with high densities of turbines began to stir concern. The iconic image of majestic birds caught in the relentless arcs of turbine blades captured public attention and demanded action. But why are these interactions occurring, and what can we do about them?

Birds typically face the most significant risks during migration, when they traverse large distances and encounter both natural and man-made obstacles. Wind turbines can be particularly hazardous for species that skim the heights where turbines operate. Certain locations, such as the migratory highways known as "flyways," intersect with ideal spots for wind farms, setting the stage for potential conflict. However, it is crucial to note that, statistically, wind turbines account for a small fraction of overall avian mortality compared to threats like habitat destruction, climate change, and, surprisingly, domestic cats.

Nevertheless, every effort to minimize wildlife impacts is essential. Enter the world of ultrasonics, radar detection, and strategic planning. Technology and research offer solutions to reduce the risk to avian populations. Advanced radar systems can now detect large flocks during peak migration periods, temporarily shutting down turbines to allow safe passage. Similarly, careful planning during the site selection phase can identify locations with lower risks to birds and bats, drastically reducing potential harm.

Bats, with their mysterious nocturnal habits and vital ecological roles, also find themselves affected by wind turbines. These creatures, often shadowy figures at dusk, are invaluable pest controllers and pollinators. However, interactions between bats and turbines can prove lethal due to a phenomenon known as "barotrauma." This occurs when bats, drawn to the turbines' moving blades, encounter sudden pressure changes that can damage their respiratory systems.

Research into bat behavior has illuminated ways to mitigate these impacts. For instance, acoustic deterrents are being developed to alter bats' echolocation signals, steering them away from danger. Moreover, adjusting turbine operation during low-wind conditions, when bats are most active, can minimize the risk of collision while having a negligible effect on energy production.

The quest for coexistence doesn't stop with birds and bats. Wind farms can also indirectly impact entire ecosystems. Construction activities, increased human presence, and infrastructure development associated with wind farms alter natural habitats. The challenge is to manage these changes thoughtfully, ensuring that the benefits of wind energy do not come at an unacceptable cost to biodiversity.

One promising approach is the integration of habitat conservation efforts with wind energy projects. This involves developing comprehensive mitigation strategies, such as creating buffer zones and restoring nearby habitats, to offset potential ecological disruptions. Some projects have succeeded in transforming adjacent areas into biodiversity reserves, providing safe havens for local wildlife while wind turbines hum in the background.

The story of the Altamont Pass in California serves as both cautionary tale and beacon of innovation. Once notorious for its high avian fatality rates, the location has become a model for mitigation and adaptation. By replacing older turbines with fewer, strategically placed modern models, the region dramatically reduced bird deaths. This success underscores the power of revisiting and revising past projects with an eye towards greater ecological sensitivity.

Engaging the community plays a critical role in fostering a harmonious relationship between wind energy projects and wildlife.   Collaborative efforts with local stakeholders, wildlife organizations, and researchers can lead to adaptive management practices that account for changing ecological dynamics and technological advances. This dialogue not only builds trust but also enriches the knowledge base, leading to more effective conservation efforts.

As we peer into the future, the relationship between wind energy and wildlife can become a model for sustainable development. The lessons learned from our past experiences and current innovations offer a roadmap for harmonizing human progress with the intricate tapestry of life on earth. Building on this foundation ensures that as we capture the winds of change, we protect the very environment from which they flow.

So, the next time we see turbines framed against the sky, let's remember that each turn of the blade represents a commitment — a commitment to clean energy, to innovation, and to a shared future where technology and nature not only coexist but thrive together. It is within our power to steer this narrative, ensuring that our pursuit of renewable energy not only benefits humanity but also honors the natural world we call home.

9.3 Noise and Aesthetic Considerations

Wind turbines, with their slender frames and majestic spin, often evoke a sense of futuristic elegance. However, as these towering sentinels dot more of our landscapes, they bring with them the undeniable presence of sound and sight. While the environmental benefits of wind energy are undisputed, the acoustics of their operation and their visual integration into the landscape spark spirited discourse. How do these gentle giants mesh with the human experience, and what does that mean for our evolving relationship with renewable energy?

To the untrained ear, a wind turbine might seem to hum along silently in the breeze. Yet, like a polite whisper at a cacophonous concert, their sound profile can be both subtle and significant. The noise emitted by wind turbines primarily stems from two sources: the mechanical hum of the machinery in the nacelle and the aerodynamic swoosh from the rotor blades slicing through the air. The latter tends to dominate, producing a rhythmic whoosh that can be heard at ground level, particularly when turbines operate at full capacity.

Perception of this noise is influenced by several factors, including distance, local topography, and ambient sound levels. For individuals living several hundred meters away, the sound might be masked by the rustling of leaves or distant traffic. However, in quieter, rural settings, the consistent presence of these sounds becomes more conspicuous. Addressing these concerns involves careful planning—placing turbines at distances far enough from residential areas to ensure that their acoustic footprint remains benign. As a general guideline, modern turbine installations strive to maintain noise levels that do not exceed ambient background levels by more than a few decibels.

Technological advancements further play a crucial role in mitigating noise. Engineers continually refine blade designs and operational mechanisms to minimize sound production. Innovations such as serrated blade edges inspired by owl wings exemplify how biomimicry helps reduce aerodynamic noise, drawing inspiration from nature to enhance engineering solutions. Additionally, regular maintenance and advancements in gearbox technology ensure that mechanical noises remain relatively subdued, emphasizing the balance between performance and quietude.

The aesthetic dimension of wind turbines is another intriguing aspect that divides public opinion. To some, these towering structures symbolize progress and ecological responsibility; to others, they are stark intrusions upon cherished vistas. This dichotomy speaks to the inherent subjectivity of aesthetic judgment. The same turbine seen as a beacon of sustainability to one observer might appear a blot on the landscape to another.

When considering landscape aesthetics, historical context provides some illumination. Human landscapes have long been arenas of change, reflecting societies' shifting values and technologies. Just as ancient stone circles and medieval cathedrals once dominated their surroundings, wind turbines are the new symbols of our age, echoing both our aspirations and our dilemmas.

To mitigate aesthetic impact, developers strive for harmony rather than dominion. Careful site selection can optimize both the energy potential and visual footprint of wind farms, integrating them into the natural environment with as little disruption as possible. In some instances, thoughtful architectural design transforms turbines into works of art, crafting projects that spark admiration rather than discomfort. Notably, the DeKo Windmill in the Netherlands doubles as an artistic installation, blurring the line between function and beauty.

Community engagement also plays a pivotal role in reconciling aesthetic concerns. Successful projects often involve collaborative dialogue with local communities, ensuring that all stakeholders have a voice in the planning process. Such interactions often lead to enhanced design solutions, fostering public goodwill and acceptance.

The narrative of noise and aesthetics within wind energy

invites us to reflect more broadly on our relationship with technology in the natural world. We inhabit landscapes sculpted by both geological time scales and human intervention; each addition is a statement of our evolving ethos. Achieving an equilibrium between energy solutions and sensory experiences challenges us to blend innovation with empathy, to walk the line between necessity and beauty.

As we navigate the expanding role of wind energy in our lives, the sound and sight of turbines prompt introspection. They remind us that while the pursuit of clean energy is paramount, the journey must incorporate the nuances of human experience. Whether viewed as elegant sentinels or mere mechanical constructs, wind turbines stand as testaments to human ingenuity, reflecting our intent to harmonize with the natural forces we harness.

Ultimately, as these sleek machines continue to grace our landscapes, they compel us to look beyond the immediate and recognize the broader tapestry they help to weave—a vision of a world powered by our renewable intentions, where the symphony of nature and technology plays on in dynamic harmony.

9.4 Land Use and Resource Management

In renewable energy, the installation of wind turbines marries the terrestrial with the ethereal, transforming air currents into a persistent hum of electricity. However, before the wind farm's blades can elegantly sweep the sky, a grounded and less poetic reality must be managed: the land that supports them. Understanding the land use and resource management aspects of wind energy is a crucial piece of this dynamic puzzle. It requires balancing the need for renewable energy development with the careful stewardship of our finite landscapes—a delicate dance mastered over years of innovation and practice.

One of the first considerations in establishing a wind farm is the physical footprint required by turbines. A single wind turbine, contrary to its towering appearance, occupies a surprisingly small amount of ground space at its base—often less than an acre. However, the space needed for an entire wind farm, including infrastructure and safe spacing between turbines to maximize efficiency and minimize turbulence, can span several acres to many square miles depending on the project scale. The placement, density, and layout of turbines are crafted meticulously to harness the best wind resources available while optimizing land use.

Historically, the open plains and windy hilltops have served as prime real estate for wind farms. These sites offer unobstructed wind paths and less ecological disruption than denser or more varied terrains might present. In the United States, states like Texas and Iowa exemplify this approach, utilizing vast swathes of agricultural land that double as sites for energy generation. This dual-use model allows farming and grazing to continue alongside energy production, adding an additional layer of resource efficiency.

However, the narrative of land use is not one of boundless expansion but rather one of strategic efficiency. Sustainable resource management emphasizes not just the quantity of land but its quality and multifunctionality. In practice, this means upholding the integrity of natural ecosystems as much as possible while installing wind farms. Buffer zones and setbacks are planned meticulously, ensuring minimal disruption to local biodiversity and protecting waterways, forests, and native vegetation from overdevelopment.

Moreover, sustainable resource management questions who benefits from land use transformation. Community involvement and benefit-sharing models have gained traction as a means to ensure that the economic fruits of wind energy are shared with those whose landscapes are altered. In some regions, community wind projects have emerged, enabling local stakeholders to take part ownership in wind energy endeavors, thereby securing not only clean energy but also economic growth for the local economy. This fosters a sense of local empowerment and ensures that land use decisions are ingrained with community consent and perspective.

The planning phase also delves into the resource management of materials used in turbine construction. While wind energy is heralded for its minimal operational emissions, the lifecycle of a wind turbine—from raw material extraction to eventual decommissioning—demands sustainable practices. The steel, fiberglass, and rare earth elements utilized in turbines highlight the need for resource efficiency from start to finish. This has catalyzed a movement towards recyclability within the industry, urging manufacturers to innovate in the use of sustainable materials and recycling protocols, thereby reducing the ecological footprint of turbine production and disposal.

Furthermore, long-term land management extends beyond the operational phase of a wind farm. Decommissioning and land restoration plans must ensure that once a turbine's life is over—typically after 20 to 25 years—the site can be reverted to its natural state or another productive use with minimal environmental cost. This forward-thinking approach seeks to mitigate long-term impacts and preserve the landscape for future generations.

Yet, despite these strategies, there remains a need for continual adaptation and learning. Adaptive management—an iterative process of implementing, monitoring, and revising management practices—plays a vital role in ensuring that wind energy development remains aligned with sustainability goals. From fine-tuning turbine placement to improving materials recycling, the ongoing feedback cycle enhances the integration of wind energy into diverse landscapes.

Perhaps the ultimate lesson of land use and resource management in wind energy is its encouragement of a broader ecological consciousness. Each wind farm not only represents a renewable energy triumph but also a commitment to responsible land stewardship. It challenges us to consider how we allocate and manage land, nudging us towards a future where energy needs are met without irrevocably altering the earth's delicate balance.

As we advance, the lessons of land use in wind energy resonate far beyond the boundaries of any single wind farm. They remind us that every decision we make—from siting turbines to embedding sustainability into resource management—forms part of an overarching narrative of harmony between human technology and the natural world. In this landscape of intersecting priorities, wind energy stands as a beacon of what is possible when sound ecological principles guide the way. The challenge is not only to install turbines that catch the wind but to craft a legacy that captures the essence of sustainable progress.

9.5 Balancing Ecosystem Preservation

As we stride confidently into an era dominated by renewable energy, the invisible threads of ecosystem preservation pull at our conscience, urging us to pause and reflect.

Wind energy, hailed for its clean credentials, also subtly challenges us to balance progress with the needs of our planet's myriad inhabitants. Navigating this tightrope requires a nuanced approach—a thoughtful blend of innovation, collaboration, and respect for nature's inherent wisdom.

The natural environment, a web of interconnected life forms and processes, offers both the resources we harness and the context within which we must operate. The challenge is how to integrate wind energy within this tapestry without unraveling its delicate fibers. Here, strategic foresight and careful planning become our allies.

The process begins long before construction crews arrive on site. It starts with meticulous environmental impact assessments, where the potential effects of proposed wind farms are measured against the backdrop of local ecosystems. This phase is critical; it is akin to laying down the first strokes on a blank canvas, determining the balance between energy goals and ecological integrity. By identifying sensitive species and habitats, assessments guide developers in avoiding critical areas and minimizing footprint size.

Consider, for example, the flourishing prairies where birds nest or coastal regions where migratory birds funnel. Avoiding these sites altogether or scheduling construction activities outside of nesting seasons are primary strategies employed to minimize disruptions to wildlife. Moreover, these decisions are not made in isolation. Collaborations with wildlife experts and environmental organizations ensure that insights from field research and ecological understanding inform sustainable project design.

Innovative approaches harness both technology and

nature-inspired solutions to mitigate impacts further. As we have discovered, adjusting turbine operations during peak wildlife activity, whether for nocturnal bats or migrating cranes, can significantly reduce potential harm. Keeping turbines static during these critical periods demonstrates the flexibility of technology when paired with ecological awareness.

At the frontier of innovation are emergent technologies, demonstrating how the digital era can aid conservation efforts. Radar systems that detect migratory bird patterns, paired with smart grid technologies, allow for real-time turbine adjustments. Such solutions underscore a broader principle: that ecological considerations are not obstacles but opportunities for sophistication and refinement in operational practices.

Yet, preserving ecosystems is not solely about abstaining from harm. It is equally about proactive restoration and enhancement. When wind projects necessitate habitat alteration, developers often follow a principle known as "biodiversity offsetting." Here, the aim is to compensate for environmental impacts by restoring or protecting another habitat of equal ecological value, creating a net-positive outcome for biodiversity.

Additionally, the notion of multi-use landscapes offers a compelling vision of coexistence. In rural areas, wind farms coexist with agricultural activities, creating a model where land supports both energy production and ecosystem services. The presence of turbines does not spell the end for local flora and fauna but invites careful integration, recognizing the land's dual potential.

Community involvement, while crucial for addressing aesthetic concerns as we have seen, plays an equally pivotal role in ecological preservation. Engaging local populations ensures that indigenous knowledge and community values inform project development. This fosters a culture of guardianship, where local stewards become partners in conservation efforts, enriching the ecological and cultural mosaic of their regions.

But perhaps the most significant strategy of all lies not in any single action but in an adaptive mindset. Ecosystems are vibrant, dynamic entities that respond to myriad pressures and changes. Adaptive management—a philosophy of learning and adjustment—ensures that as our understanding of local ecologies deepens, so does our capacity to fine-tune our approach. This continual feedback loop between observation and action is the hallmark of true ecological stewardship.

Amidst this web of strategies and solutions, an underlying truth persists: wind energy, like all human endeavor, imparts changes upon the world. The goal, then, is not merely to avoid harm, but to foster a harmonious existence where energy production enriches rather than diminishes the natural world.

As we advance into the future, balancing ecosystem preservation with energy goals becomes more than just a project requirement; it becomes a reflection of our values as a society. It challenges us to envision not just what we can achieve through technology, but how that technology interacts with life in its many forms.

So let us navigate this path with humility and ambition, crafting a legacy that celebrates not only the wind turbines on the horizon but the myriad life that inhabits the lands below. When we strike this balance, we honor not just our present needs but the enduring richness of life, stewarding a planet that future generations—and all its inhabitants—will be grateful to inherit.

Chapter 10

Wind Energy Policy and Economics

Wind energy policy involves incentives and regulations that drive sector growth, while addressing economic hurdles like production costs and market barriers. Investment interest is spurred by technological advancements and supportive frameworks. Comparing global policies reveals diverse approaches to fostering wind energy, impacting its expansion. Addressing these economic and regulatory aspects is crucial for the sustainable development and competitiveness of wind energy in the global market.

10.1   Government Incentives and Regulations

Government incentives and regulations act as both the cheerleaders and referees of the wind energy sector, driving its development while ensuring it remains a fair player on the economic and environmental stage. These policy mechanisms are pivotal for catalyzing the growth of wind energy, especially in its nascent stages, where market forces alone might flounder.

The inception of government policies to spur wind energy can be traced back to the 1970s, a period when energy crises flustered the world and the quest for renewable energy sources gained traction. This sparked the initial wave of support mechanisms like subsidies, tax incentives, and public investment, laying down the cornerstones of the industry's modern structure.

Subsidies and Tax Incentives

Subsidies serve as a direct financial aid to cover some of the costs involved in the production and installation of wind energy technologies. For instance, the Production Tax Credit (PTC) in the United States has been a monumental pillar for wind power expansion. Initially established under the Energy Policy Act of 1992, the PTC provides a per-kilowatt-hour tax credit for the electricity generated by qualified wind projects.

In Europe, Feed-in Tariffs (FiTs) have historically been a popular incentive mechanism. Countries like Germany led the charge with schemes that guaranteed a fixed premium price for electricity generated from wind, ensuring steady revenue for investors and developers. While the PTC and FiTs may differ in mechanics, both instill confidence in investors by mitigating financial risks, thus accelerating deployment.

Tax incentives, such as investment tax credits, also play a crucial role. These credits allow wind energy producers to deduct a percentage of investment costs from their tax liabilities, immediately easing the financial burden. Such fiscal relief has been instrumental in transforming mere ideas into towering turbines dotting the landscape.

Renewable Portfolio Standards

Beyond subsidies, regulatory frameworks such as Renewable Portfolio Standards (RPS) compel utilities to source a certain percentage of their electricity from renewable resources like wind. This obligatory target not only creates a robust demand for wind energy but also fosters competitiveness among different energy technologies.

For example, Texas, often associated more with oil than wind, implemented its RPS in the late 1990s. Remarkably, the state now leads the United States in wind energy capacity, illustrating how regulatory mandates can shift energy landscapes. By setting clear goals and timelines, RPS encourages coalitions of stakeholders—including state agencies, utilities, and the wind industry—to collaborate in meeting statutory benchmarks.

Carbon Pricing and Cap-and-Trade Programs

As societies increasingly acknowledge the environmental impacts of fossil fuels, carbon pricing emerges as an effective policy tool to incentivize renewables. By attaching a cost to carbon emissions, these programs inherently make clean energy solutions like wind more attractive. Cap-and-trade schemes, where a capped amount of emission allowances can be traded in a market system, exemplify this approach.

The European Union Emission Trading Scheme (EU ETS), initiated in 2005, serves as a prime example where wind energy not only provides a means to meet climate targets but also gains a competitive edge as industries seek cost-effective ways to reduce their carbon footprint.

Permit and Zoning Regulations

While incentives are vital, regulations that govern land use and permitting processes can significantly impact wind energy projects. Streamlining these procedures is essential to avoid bureaucratic bottlenecks that can stall progress. Ensuring that zoning laws amicably balance the needs of communities with the development of wind farms can pave the way for smoother project

161

implementations.

Some countries have pioneered innovative regulatory frameworks to address these challenges. Denmark, for instance, has implemented a proactive approach where potential wind farm sites are pre-screened for environmental and zoning suitability, significantly expediting the approval process once developers submit formal applications.

The Global Policy Context

On a global scale, the adoption of the Paris Agreement in 2015 marked a collective effort to combat climate change, underscoring the impetus for renewables, including wind energy. Various international initiatives, like the International Renewable Energy Agency (IRENA), offer platforms for countries to collaborate on policy frameworks that stimulate wind energy development.

Comparative examples reveal a spectrum of approaches. China's state-driven massive wind power expansion program contrasts with Australia's mix of market-based mechanisms and regional commitments, indicating that while the paths may differ, the wind energy goal remains shared.

Challenges in Implementation

Despite the promise of these initiatives, challenges abound. Policy stability remains a perennial concern, as frequent changes can deter investment by creating an unpredictable business environment. Furthermore, integrating wind power into existing energy grids poses technical challenges, requiring coordinated efforts in grid management and technological innovations.

Moreover, while incentives aim to address economic barriers, ensuring equitable access to these benefits remains a crucial consideration. Small and medium-sized enterprises, particularly in developing regions, may struggle without sufficient governmental support or access to financing.

Future Outlook

Looking ahead, the alignment of government policies with technological innovations, such as offshore wind and energy storage solutions, presents promising avenues for wind energy's future. As climate impacts become more profound, the urgency to enhance and optimize policy tools to foster wind energy intensifies.

Government incentives and regulations function as both catalysts and guardians of wind energy's growth. Their efficacy in marrying environmental sustainability with economic viability is fundamental to the sector's success. As the winds of change continue to blow, crafting dynamic and adaptive policy landscapes will be key to harnessing nature's power sustainably and efficiently.

10.2 Cost of Wind Energy Production

The economic landscape of wind energy production is as dynamic as the breezes it harnesses, with costs experiencing swift shifts akin to weather changes. Understanding these costs provides insight not only into the feasibility of wind as a renewable energy source but also into the strategic decisions that shape its deployment.

Capital Expenditure (CapEx)

The journey of wind energy begins with a substantial initial investment, known in financial lexicon as Capital Expenditure (CapEx). This encompasses a variety of tangible components—turbines, towers, blades, transformers—and intangibles such as site preparation and planning. Unsurprisingly, the turbines themselves gobble up the largest share of CapEx, typically accounting for about 70% of the total. This isn't just a splurge on whirligigs; rather, it's a commitment to advanced technology designed to extract maximum energy efficiently over decades.

But before the turbines can greet the sky, substantial groundwork is necessary. This involves site evaluation, environmental assessments, and securing permits—not to mention a considerable amount of good ol' fashioned paperwork. Herein lies a paradox: while wind is free, getting to the point where you can utilize it requires a cash outlay reminiscent of erecting a skyscraper.

Practical examples illustrate variations in costs based on geographic and technological factors. For instance, offshore wind farms, celebrated for their stronger and more consistent winds, bear higher installation costs compared to their landlocked counterparts due to more complex infrastructure needs. Yet, their potential for higher energy yield often tips the economic scales in their favor over time.

Operating Expenditure (OpEx)

Once the turbines are up and spinning, the focus shifts to Operating Expenditure (OpEx), the recurring cost that keeps the gears turning smoothly over the lifespan of the wind farm. OpEx includes maintenance, land lease payments, insurance, and administrative costs. Unlike a temperamental antique car, wind turbines are designed to require minimal but routine TLC (turbine-loving care).

Maintenance expenses generally hinge on the age and technology used. Newer models, with sleeker, more sophisticated designs, often demand less upkeep. Advances in materials and design have led to more robust blades and towers, reducing unforeseen maintenance costs over time.

Interestingly, the industry's maturation has also given rise to predictive maintenance, a strategy that uses real-time data and analytics to preemptively address issues before they become costly repairs. This proactive approach not only curtails OpEx but also enhances the reliability and efficiency of wind energy production.

Levelized Cost of Energy (LCOE)

To make sense of these financial facets, the Levelized Cost of Energy (LCOE) emerges as a vital metric. It essentially distills the total cost of building and operating a wind farm over its assumed lifespan into a single measure, expressed as cost per kilowatt-hour (kWh) produced. Metaphorically, it's like the long-term average cost of a coffee maker per cup of joe, factoring in both purchase and brewing costs.

Historically, the LCOE for wind energy has exhibited a downward trajectory, signaling increasing affordability. Between 2009 and 2020 alone, the cost per kWh for wind energy fell by approximately 70%, attributable largely to technological advancements, economies of scale, and competitive supply chains.

Economic Viability and Challenges

Despite wind energy's cost declines, economic viability doesn't solely hinge on LCOE. The dynamics of energy markets, subsidy structures, and energy demand shape the financial landscape. Power Purchase Agreements (PPAs) often anchor wind energy projects, offering long-term contracts that hedge against market volatility and provide stable revenue streams.

Nevertheless, challenges loom. As wind energy penetrates the grid further, issues such as grid integration costs and variability management need addressing. Yet, technological innovations, like energy storage systems and improved grid management strategies, continue to bolster the economic case for wind energy.

Case Study: The Danish Experience

Denmark, a global wind energy leader, exemplifies the fusion of policy and economic pragmatism. The nation's concerted efforts to streamline both CapEx and OpEx have propelled it to the forefront of wind energy. Denmark's strategic investments in research, coupled with supportive policies, have not only spurred domestic wind farm growth but have also catalyzed a thriving export industry.

The symbiosis of private sector ingenuity and public sector facilitation has created a fertile ground for lower LCOEs, enabling Denmark to achieve one of the highest market shares of wind-sourced electricity globally.

Future Prospects

Looking beyond the horizon, the trajectory of wind energy production costs continues to follow a promising path. Innovations such as larger, more efficient turbines, floating offshore platforms, and enhanced materials forecasting further reductions in LCOE. As economies of scale and competitive markets drive costs down, wind energy inches closer to its potential as a dominant global energy source.

The cost of wind energy production straddles an intriguing balance of initial heft and long-term savings. As operational efficiencies improve and technology advances, the vision of affordable, sustainable energy inches ever closer to reality. Wind energy's economic narrative, punctuated by innovation and policy, remains a testament to the human capacity to harness nature's complexity for the collective good.

10.3 Market Dynamics and Investment

As the sails of wind energy unfurl across the globe, understanding the market dynamics and investment landscape becomes as intriguing as riding the zephyrs themselves. The wind energy market, propelled by a confluence of environmental imperatives and technological advances, offers fertile ground for both challenges and opportunities. Investors and policymakers alike are venturing beyond the turbine blades, seeking to grasp the economic forces driving this vibrant sector.

Supply and Demand Dynamics

At its heart, the wind energy market operates like any classic economic model, dancing to the tunes of supply and demand. However, this melody is harmonized by a unique set of players and circumstances. As society's appetite for cleaner energy sources grows, the demand for wind energy is soaring to unprecedented heights.

But demand alone does not compose a symphony; supply must rise to the occasion. Here, technological breakthroughs—such as advancements in turbine efficiency and energy storage—play a crucial role in elevating supply capabilities. Coupled with decreasing production costs, highlighted by the Levelized Cost of Energy (LCOE) approach from previous discussions, the supply side of wind energy enjoys a serendipitous boost.

Moreover, policy incentives remain integral to this balance, akin to a seasoned conductor ensuring harmony. Government frameworks often dictate market conditions by incentivizing supply, as seen with production tax credits and feed-in tariffs, spurring investment into infrastructure that sustains upward momentum.

167

Investment Considerations

The quest for the golden mean of sustainable investment hinges on diverse factors. One major consideration is the geographical dispersion of wind resources. Investors are keenly aware that not all breezes are created equal. Coastal and offshore regions often promise higher yields, offering investors a gustier return on investment. However, investments in offshore projects require deep pockets, prompting a varied portfolio strategy comprising both onshore and offshore ventures.

Moreover, investors must navigate the intricate maze of regulation and policy. Shifts in national energy policies can drastically alter market attractiveness, positioning stability as a prized investment criteria. Investing in wind energy, therefore, is akin to mastering the unpredictable moves of a wind vane—constantly aligning with policy shifts, technological innovations, and market trends.

Risk Management and Mitigation

As with any windfall opportunity, there comes an element of risk. Wind energy investments grapple with challenges such as fluctuating energy prices, technological reliability, and grid integration dilemmas. Here lies the ingenuity of risk mitigation strategies: Power Purchase Agreements (PPAs) often emerge as risk hedges, facilitating long-term price stability and revenue predictability for investors.

In parallel, leveraging insurance and financial products designed for renewables can cushion against unforeseen setbacks, adding an extra layer of stability. Additionally, the maturation of markets has fostered sophisticated financial instruments, such as green bonds and energy derivatives, offering innovative avenues for risk management and investment optimization.

168

Financing the Future

The financing of wind energy ventures presents a lucrative tableau for economic growth. Diverse financing models, from traditional bank loans to venture capital and public-private partnerships, sketch a broad canvas of possibilities. Green bonds, in particular, have become an artful means of attracting socially responsible investments, linking capital markets to sustainable energy projects.

One cannot overlook the role of international finance in orchestrating the wind energy movement. Global financial institutions often underpin large-scale projects in emerging markets, here deploying their vast resources to bridge the investment gap. Examples abound; consider the World Bank's support for wind projects in Africa and Asia, underscoring the transnational nature of wind energy finance.

Case Study: China's Wind Energy Surge

Examining China sheds light on the crux of market dynamics and investment strategy. As the world's largest wind energy producer, China's market offers a rich tapestry of lessons for investors. Through state-driven incentives and robust supply chain capacity, China has effectively scaled up its wind energy capabilities. This reflects the growing symbiosis between national ambition and global market forces—a paradigm of how policy, supply chain, and financing collaborate to create a giant in the wind energy sector.

China's experience showcases an intriguing investment dichotomy: while governmental backing reduces market volatility, it also necessitates adept navigation of bureaucratic channels for investment success. Therefore, while global investors eagerly partake in this market, local partnerships and insights prove crucial to unlocking

169

its full potential.

Technological Impacts on Market Dynamics

Technology continues to weave its transformative tapestry over the market. Breakthroughs in digitalization, such as data analytics and predictive maintenance, not only improve operational efficiency but also enhance investment attractiveness. By increasing reliability and performance, these innovations tip the scales in favor of wind energy as a sound investment.

Moreover, the development of complementary technologies like battery storage and smart grid solutions further solidify the viability of wind power, offsetting intermittency issues and facilitating smoother grid integration. These advancements symbolize the forward motion of wind energy, thrusting the market confidently into an era dominated by innovation-infused strategies.

The Road Ahead

Navigating the market dynamics and investment potential of wind energy is a journey as exhilarating as a free-wheeling breeze. It requires foresight, adaptability, and a keen understanding of the intricate dance between policy, technology, and market forces. Much like the wind itself, opportunities in this arena are boundless, waiting to be harnessed by those bold enough to embrace the challenge.

10.4 Barriers to Entry and Industry Challenges

Entering the wind energy sector might feel like setting sail amidst formidable gales; the journey promises bountiful rewards, yet the obstacles can seem insurmountable. For aspiring players in this green frontier, understanding the economic barriers and industry-specific challenges is critical to plotting a successful course.

High Initial Capital Investment

A towering barrier for newcomers is the substantial initial capital required to launch wind energy projects. The hefty costs of purchasing, installing, and commissioning wind turbines, along with the requisite infrastructure, demand significant funding sources. Unlike swashbuckling ventures that thrive on modest entry outlays, the wind energy industry necessitates a robust financial foundation.

Acquiring such capital can be especially daunting for small and medium-sized enterprises (SMEs), which often struggle to secure financing without established credit histories or collateral. This contrasts sharply with wind energy behemoths whose coffers are sustained by ample reserves and easier access to credit. Thus, many potential new entrants are left navigating a financial thicket, foraging for ways to scale the capital mountain.

Regulatory and Permitting Hurdles

As straightforward as it seems to harness breezes, the regulatory process is anything but breezy. Obtaining permits involves intricate, time-consuming processes, including environmental assessments, community consultations, and land use agreements. These legal and bureaucratic mazes can delay projects for years, increasing the financial burden on budding enthusiasts.

Particularly in markets with stringent environmental regulations, even the most ambition-fueled entrant may find their progress stalled by red tape. Navigating through these hurdles requires not only persistence but also a deft understanding of national and local legislation—a task often better suited to seasoned industry players with established legal teams.

Access to Technology and Expertise

Access to cutting-edge technology and technical expertise is another formidable challenge. New entrants must equip themselves with the latest turbine technology and operational know-how to compete effectively. However, acquiring this equipment can be prohibitively expensive, and cultivating technical prowess takes time and resources.

Larger, well-established companies typically benefit from economies of scale and global supply chain networks, allowing them to outpace smaller competitors in securing advanced technologies. Additionally, the increasing complexity of wind energy solutions demands that entrants invest in skilled labor, which can be scarce and expensive due to high industry demand.

Market Competition and Saturation

Targeting markets with established players introduces further hurdles. Entrants face competition from companies that have honed their craft, optimized operations, and developed proprietary technologies over decades. These incumbents possess strategic advantages, from well-oiled supply chains to fortified customer relationships, often resulting in a competitive edge that can dwarf novice aspirations.

In some regions, market saturation exacerbates competitive pressures. For example, countries leading in wind energy capacity may witness slowed growth prospects due to limited available sites and heightened competition for prime locations. This saturation can discourage new investment and stimulate fierce price wars, reducing margins for all but the most efficient operators.

Policy Uncertainty

While policies have been discussed as catalysts for growth, their fickle nature sometimes acts as a deterrent. Policy uncertainty—caused by sudden shifts in government incentives, renewable energy targets, or tax regimes—can create an inconsistent playing field, rendering financial modeling and strategic planning akin to reading tea leaves. New entrants craving predictability may find policy shifts destabilizing, discouraging them from making substantial commitments.

Grid Integration and Infrastructure Development

Beyond business fundamentals, logistical challenges loom. Integrating wind energy into national grids requires advances in infrastructure. Entrants must consider the costs and risks associated with connecting to transmission lines, which may not be readily available or sufficiently robust to handle new capacity.

Additionally, intermittent power supply, synonymous with wind energy, necessitates comprehensive grid management solutions to stabilize output. This often involves investment in complementary technologies like energy storage, further elevating entry costs.

Navigating the Challenges: Strategic Insights

Despite the headwinds, innovative strategies can help new entrants gain a foothold in the industry. Collaboration emerges as a beacon of potential; partnerships with established entities, through joint ventures or strategic alliances, can ameliorate technology and capital access issues. Engaging in consortia allows entrants to share resources, mitigate risks, and collectively surmount regulatory hurdles.

Embracing niche markets or niche technologies also offers a pathway to success. By focusing on specific geographic areas or innovative solutions, entrants can carve distinct market positions free from direct competition with industry giants.

Lastly, sustainable practices can be a differentiator. As global knowledge concerning climate impact grows, the demand for environmentally considerate brands rises in tandem. Entrants that prioritize sustainability, both in operations and supply chains, may find themselves growing popular with conscientious consumers and investors.

The wind energy industry, while rife with opportunities, is peppered with entry barriers and operational challenges. From high initial costs and regulatory complexities to technology access and fierce competition, newcomers must navigate a labyrinth of hurdles to succeed.

Yet, armed with strategic acumen, collaborative spirit, and a commitment to sustainability, these aspiring adventurers can harness the wind's power to propel their ventures toward a future teeming with promise. Rolling with the changing gusts, they may transform barriers into bridges, bolstered by an energetic resolve to succeed where others may falter. The winds of opportunity await those daring enough to weather the industry's formidable challenges with courage, innovation, and tenacity.

10.5   Global   Comparison   of   Wind Energy Policies

As the world rallies around the banners of sustainability and energy transition, wind energy emerges as a frontline contender in the global race toward renewable integration. Yet, the policies nurturing this momentum vary dramatically, much like the winds they seek to harness. These policies, sculpted by economic imperatives and environmental commitments, shape not only the deployment speed but also the technological direction of wind energy.

United States: A Patchwork of Policies

The United States offers a mosaic of wind energy policies as diverse as its landscapes. Federal incentives like the Production Tax Credit (PTC) have historically been instrumental in spurring investment, yet these are complemented—or complicated—by a carousel of state-specific policies.

Renewable Portfolio Standards (RPS) present a fascinating element, as states independently determine long-term clean energy targets, creating a decentralized but competitive policy environment. Texas, for instance, turned heads by achieving the largest installed wind capacity, driven by robust RPS and astute grid management strategies.

However, the U.S. also exemplifies how policy discontinuity, such as the expiration and renewal cycles of the PTC, introduces periods of uncertainty, potentially stalling new projects and complicating investment decisions.

European Union: A Collective Commitment

Across the Atlantic, the European Union exemplifies a more coordinated approach. The EU's climate and energy framework mandates binding renewable energy targets for member states, fostering pan-European solidarity in clean energy adoption. This collective ambition is anchored by market-based mechanisms like the EU Emissions Trading System (ETS), driving wind energy growth through carbon pricing.

175

The feed-in tariff success story in Germany highlights how stable, long-term pricing contracts can energize the industry. Germany's pioneering efforts under the Erneuerbare-Energien-Gesetz (Renewable Energy Act) transformed the nation into a wind powerhouse, though recent shifts to competitive auctions reflect evolving policy sophistication aimed at lowering costs.

China: Commanding Heights

China personifies the scale combined with state-driven coordination. As the world's largest wind energy market, it benefits from a unique blend of national directives and financial incentives, epitomizing large-scale deployment. China's five-year plans methodically incorporate renewable energy objectives, ensuring alignment across policy, industry, and financing channels.

Notably, China's success lies in pairing stringent mandates with formidable public investment, orchestrating a rapid scale-up of both onshore and offshore wind capacities. The country leverages its manufacturing prowess to generate a cascading effect, reducing equipment costs that further accelerates deployment domestically and internationally.

India: Ambition Meets Complexity

In India, wind energy policies blend ambition with complexity. The national goal of installing 60 GW of wind capacity by 2022 spotlighted government intention, yet the decentralization of energy policy entails coordination challenges.

States like Tamil Nadu and Gujarat seize leadership roles, pioneering competitive auctions and favorable land policies to attract investment. However, infrastructure limitations and financial bottlenecks remain hurdles, nudging policymakers towards more cohesive national frameworks to fully realize their renewable energy aspirations.

Australia: Renewable Riches Amidst Political Flux

Australia presents a paradox of renewable riches amidst political flux. The country possesses some of the world's best wind resources but has struggled with policy consistency. Federal-level tensions and changing renewable energy targets contribute to periods of uncertainty, impeding investor confidence.

Despite these challenges, states like South Australia have forged ahead with bold renewable targets and battery storage integration, demonstrating subnational leadership. Such instances underscore how state-level innovation can counterbalance federal vacillation in policy efficacy.

Nordic Nations: Wind with Synergy

In the Nordic nations, wind energy policies intertwine with a rich tapestry of hydropower and efficient grid systems. Denmark deserves special mention, having shown that national ambition, public-private partnerships, and community involvement can harmonize to amplify wind energy's role drastically.

Denmark's emphasis on public acceptance and ecologically mindful deployment serves as a model for integrating renewable projects into the social fabric, easing the transition process.

Emerging Markets: New Frontiers

In emerging markets, diverse strategies reveal the undercurrents of local conditions. South Africa has implemented the Renewable Energy Independent Power Producer Procurement Programme (REIPPPP), catalyzing an impressive build-out of wind infrastructure via transparent, competitive auctions that have attracted foreign investment.

Brazil embraces its vast wind potential through auction systems that ensure competitive electricity prices and enduring contracts. These policies nurture investor confidence and inspire replication in other regions seeking efficient modal shifts to renewables.

Policy Influence on Technology

Beyond borders, national wind energy policies also steer technological innovations. Offshore wind technologies, for instance, have flourished in countries possessing coherent strategies and generous subsidies, such as the UK and China, driving down costs through economies of scale and technological advancements.

Policy-driven incentives for research and development can influence not only the pace of technological innovation but also a nation's standing in the global energy sphere. Integrating wind energy into hybrid renewable models, encompassing storage and smart grid technology, stimulates investment in cutting-edge solutions to overcome intermittency and grid challenges.

Lessons and Pathways Forward

The wind energy sector teaches lessons that transcend geography: the effectiveness of policies reflects in their stability, predictability, and adaptability. As climate imperatives gather momentum, governments must weave adaptable, long-term strategies into the fabric of their clean energy transition plans.

Overall, whether through singular focus or regional collaboration, the world's myriad wind policies collectively embody an acknowledgment that the path to sustainable energy is a mutual journey. As nations peer beyond the wind-blown horizon, let us hope they learn from one another and draw inspiration from the policies that energize the planet—one innovation, one barrier solved at a time.